Fodor's New Pocket Prague

D0067004

Parts of this book appear in
Fodor's Eastern Europe

Fodor's Travel Publications, Inc.
New York • Toronto • London •
Sydney • Auckland

First Edition

ISBN 0–679–03104–9

Fodor's Pocket Prague

Editor: Christopher Billy
Contributors: Steven K. Amsterdam, Mark Baker, William Echikson, Ky Krauthamer, Martha Lagace, Delia Meth-Cohn
Creative Director: Fabrizio La Rocca
Cartographer: David Lindroth
Illustrator: Karl Tanner
Cover Photograph: Glen Allison/Tony Stone Images
Design: Vignelli Associates

Special Sales

Contents

Contents iv

Maps and Plans

Foreword

While every care has been taken to ensure the accuracy of the information in this guide, the passage of time will always bring change, and consequently, the publisher cannot accept responsibility for errors that may occur.

All prices and opening times quoted here are based on information supplied to us at press time. Hours and admission fees may change, however, and the prudent traveler will avoid inconvenience by calling ahead.

Fodor's wants to hear about your travel experiences, both pleasant and unpleasant. When a hotel or restaurant fails to live up to its billing, let us know, and we will investigate the complaint and revise our entries where the facts warrant it.

Send your letters to the editors of Fodor's Travel Publications, 201 East 50th Street, New York, NY 10022.

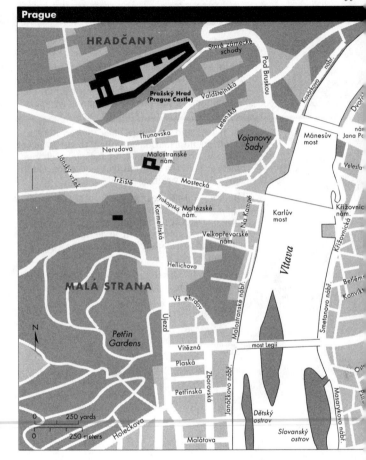

Prague

HRADČANY

Staré zámecké schody

Pod Bruskou

Kožátkovo nábř.

Dvoř·

Pražský Hrad
(Prague Castle)

Valdštejnská

Letenská

Thunovská

Vojanovy
Šady

Mánesův
most

nám
Jana Po·

Nerudova

Malostranské
nám.

Jánský vršek

Tržiště

Mostecká

Velesla·

Na Kampě

Prokopská Maltézské
nám.

Karlův
most

Křižovnic
nám.

Karmelitská

Velkopřevorské
nám.

Vltava

Křižovnická

Hellichova

Betlém·

MALÁ STRANA

Vš ehrdov

Smetanovo nábř.

Konvik·

Újezd

Malostranské nábř.

N

Petřin
Gardens

Vítězná

most Legií

Plaská

Zborovská

Janáčkovo nábř.

Ost·

Petřínská

Masarykovo nábř.

Pa·

0   250 yards

0   250 meters

Holečkova

Malátova

Dětský
ostrov

Slovanský
ostrov

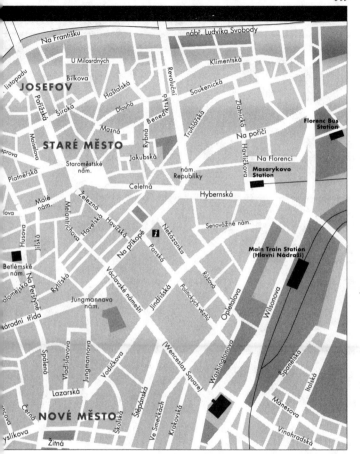

Czech Republic

GERMANY

Dresden
Görlitz
Wroclaw

Chemnitz

Děčín
Liberec
Ústí
Jablonec
Teplice
Česká Lípa
Most
Litoměřice
Chomutov
Louny
Mladá
Boleslav
Náchod
Karlovy
Vary
E48
E55
E65
Hradec Králové
Kladno
Cheb
E67
Kolín
Pardubice
Marjánské Lázně
Beroun
Prague
Chrudim
Kutná
Hora
Plzeň
E50
BOHEMIA
Svitávy
Příbram
Vlašim
E53
Milevsko
Tábor
Havlíčkův
Brod
Olom
E49
Jihlava
Proste
Klatovy
Písek
Brno
E461
Strakonice
Telč
Uherské
Třeboň
Český
Krumlov
České
Budějovice
Znojmo
Břeclav

N

GERMANY

Vienna

0   60 miles
0   90 km

AUSTRIA

Bratisla

Introduction

By Mark Baker and Delia Meth-Cohn

We are living in the Left Bank of the '90s," wrote Alan Levy, the editor in chief of the *Prague Post*, for the newspaper's debut edition in 1991. With those few words, Levy gave rise to one of the sweetest myths to grace the postrevolutionary period in Eastern Europe. Prague isn't really the modern equivalent of 1920s Paris, but the characterization isn't wholly inaccurate either. Like all other good myths, whether grounded in fact or fantasy, the belief that something special is happening here has achieved some measure of truth through sheer repetition and force of will. By hook or by crook, Prague has become, well, quite Bohemian in its own way.

In the five years since Prague's students took to the streets to help bring down the 40-year-old communist regime, the city has enjoyed an unparalleled cultural renaissance. Much of the energy has come from planeloads of idealistic young Americans, but the enthusiasm has been shared in near-equal measure by their Czech counterparts and by the many newcomers who have arrived from all over the world. Amid Prague's cobblestone streets and gold-tipped spires, new galleries, cafés, and clubs teem with bright-eyed "expatriates" and perplexed locals who must wonder how their city came to be Eastern Europe's new Left Bank. New shops and, perhaps most noticeably, scads of new restaurants have recently opened up, expanding the city's culinary reach far beyond the traditional roast pork and dumplings. Many have something to learn in the way of presentation and service, but Praguers still marvel at a variety that was unthinkable only a few years ago.

The arts and theater are also thriving in the "new" Prague. Young playwrights, some writing in English, regularly stage their own works. Weekly poetry readings are standing-room-only. The city's dozen or so rock clubs are jammed nightly; bands play everything from metal and psychedelic to garage and grunge.

All of this frenetic activity plays well against a stunning backdrop of towering churches and centuries-old bridges and alleyways. Prague achieved much of its present glory during the 14th century, during the long reign of Charles IV, king of Bohemia and Moravia, and Holy Roman Emperor. It was Charles who established a university in the city and laid out the New Town (Nové Město), charting Prague's growth.

During the 15th century, the city's development was hampered by the Hussite Wars, a series of crusades launched by the Holy Roman Empire to subdue the fiercely independent Czech noblemen. The Czechs were eventually defeated in 1620 at the Battle of White Mountain (Bílá Hora) near Prague and were ruled by the Habsburg family for the next 300 years. Under the Habsburgs, Prague became a German-speaking city and an important administrative center, but it was forced to play second fiddle to the monarchy's capitol of Vienna. Much of the Lesser Town (Malá Strana), across the river, was built up at this time, becoming home to Austrian nobility and its Baroque tastes.

Prague regained its status as a national capitol in 1918, with the creation of the modern Czechoslovak state, and quickly asserted itself in the interwar period as a vital cultural center. Although the city escaped World War II essentially intact, it and the rest of Czechoslovakia fell under the political and cultural domination of the Soviet Union until the 1989 popular uprisings that ended the 40-year reign of the country's pro-Soviet government. The election of dissident playwright Václav Havel to the post of national president in June 1990 set the stage for the city's renaissance, which has since proceeded at a dizzying, quite Bohemian rate.

1 Essential Information

Before You Go

Government Tourist Offices

Čedok, the official travel bureau for the Czech Republic and Slovakia, is actually a travel agent rather than a tourist information office. It will supply you with hotel and travel information, and book air and rail tickets for travel within either country, but don't expect much in the way of general information.

In the United States: 10 E. 40th St., New York, NY 10016, tel. 212/689–9720. **In the United Kingdom:** 17–18 Old Bond St., London W1X 4RB, tel. 0171/629–6058.

When to Go

Prague is beautiful year-round, but avoid midsummer (especially July and August) and the Christmas and Easter holidays, when the city is overrun with tourists. Spring and fall generally combine good weather with a more bearable level of tourism. During the winter months you'll encounter few other visitors and have the opportunity to see Prague breathtakingly covered in snow; but many of the sights are closed, and it can get very cold. The same guidelines generally apply to traveling in the rest of Bohemia and Moravia, although even in high season (August), the number of visitors to these areas is far smaller than in Prague. The Giant Mountains of Bohemia come into their own in winter (December–February), when skiers from all over the country crowd the slopes and resorts. If you're not into skiing, try visiting the mountains in late spring (May or June) or fall, when the colors are dazzling and you'll have the hotels and restaurants pretty much to yourself. Bear in mind that many castles and museums are closed November through March.

Climate The following are the average daily maximum and minimum temperatures for Prague.

Prague							
Jan.	36F	2C	**May**	66F	19C	**Sept.**	68F 20C
	25	−4		46	8		50 10
Feb.	37F	3C	**June**	72F	22C	**Oct.**	55F 13C
	27	−3		52	11		41 5
Mar.	46F	8C	**July**	75F	24C	**Nov.**	46F 8C
	32	0		55	13		36 2
Apr.	58F	14C	**Aug.**	73F	23C	**Dec.**	37F 3C
	39	4		55	13		28 −2

Information Sources For current weather conditions and forecasts for cities in the United States and abroad, as well as the local time and helpful travel tips, call the **Weather Channel Connection** (tel. 900/932–8437; 95¢ per minute) from a touch-tone phone.

What to Pack

In the postcommunist Czech Republic, Western dress of any kind is considered stylish, so don't bother bringing your tuxedo. A sports jacket for men, and a dress or pants for women, is appropriate for an evening out in Prague or in the better Bohemian spa towns. Everywhere else, you'll feel comfortable in casual corduroys or jeans. Most of the country is best seen on foot, so take a pair of sturdy walking shoes and be prepared to use them. Throughout Eastern Europe, high heels present a considerable problem on cobblestone streets, and Prague is no exception. If you plan to visit the mountains, make sure your shoes have good traction and ankle support, as some trails can be quite challenging. Many consumer goods are still in short supply. Be sure to bring any medications or special toiletries you may require. You will need an electrical adapter for small appliances; the voltage is 220, with 50 cycles.

Miscellaneous Many items that you take for granted at home are occasionally unavailable or of questionable quality in Eastern Europe. Take your own toiletries and personal-hygiene products with you. Women should pack tampons or sanitary napkins, which are in chronic short supply. Few places provide sports equipment for rent; an alternative to bringing your own equipment would be to buy what you need locally and take it home with you. In general, sporting goods are relatively cheap and of good quality. Bring an extra pair of eyeglasses or contact lenses in your carry-on luggage. If you have a health problem that requires a prescription drug, pack enough of the medication to last the duration of the trip or have your doctor write a prescription using the drug's generic name, because brand names vary from one country to another. Always carry prescription drugs in their original packaging to avoid problems with customs officials. Don't pack them in luggage that you plan to check in case your bags go astray. In addition, pack a list of the offices that supply refunds for lost or stolen traveler's checks.

Electricity The electrical current in Eastern Europe is 220 volts, 50 cycles alternating current (AC); the United States runs on 110-volt, 60-cycle AC current. Unlike wall outlets in the United States, which accept plugs with two flat prongs, outlets in Eastern Europe generally take plugs with three prongs, although some older establishments may use 110 volts.

Adapters,
Converters,
Transformers
To use U.S.-made electrical appliances abroad, you'll need an adapter plug. Unless the appliance is dual-voltage and made for travel, you'll also need a converter. Hotels sometimes have 110-volt outlets for low-wattage appliances marked FOR SHAVERS ONLY near the sink; don't use them for a high-wattage appliance like a blow-dryer. If you're traveling with an old laptop computer, carry a transformer. New laptop computers are auto-sensing, operating equally well on 110 and 220 volts (so you need only the appropriate adapter plug). When in doubt, consult your owner's manual or the manufacturer. Or get a copy of the free brochure "Foreign Electricity is No Deep Dark Secret," published by adapter-converter manufacturer Franzus Company (Customer Service, Dept. B50, Murtha Industrial Park, Box 142, Beacon Falls, CT 06403, tel. 203/723–6664).

Luggage
Regulations
Free airline baggage allowances depend on the airline, the route, and the class of your ticket; ask in advance. In general, on domestic flights and on international flights between the United States and foreign destinations, you are entitled to check two bags—neither exceeding 62 inches,

or 158 centimeters (length + width + height), or weighing more than 70 pounds (32 kilograms). A third piece may be brought aboard; its total dimensions are generally limited to less than 45 inches (114 centimeters), so it will fit easily under the seat in front of you or in the overhead compartment. In the United States, the Federal Aviation Administration gives airlines broad latitude to limit carry-on allowances and tailor them to different aircraft and operational conditions. Charges for excess, oversize, or overweight pieces vary.

If you are flying between two foreign destinations, note that baggage allowances may be determined not by piece but by weight, which generally allows 88 pounds (40 kilograms) of luggage in first class, 66 pounds (30 kilograms) in business class, and 44 pounds (20 kilograms) in economy. If your flight between two cities abroad *connects* with your transatlantic or transpacific flight, the piece method still applies.

Safeguarding Your Luggage Before leaving home, itemize your bags' contents and their worth in case they go astray. To minimize that risk, tag them inside and out with your name, address, and phone number. (If you use your home address, cover it so that potential thieves can't see it.) Put a copy of your itinerary inside each bag so that you can be tracked easily. At check-in, make sure the tag attached by baggage handlers bears the correct three-letter code for your destination. If your bags do not arrive with you, or if you detect damage, immediately file a written report with the airline before you leave the airport.

Czech Currency

The unit of currency in the Czech Republic is the koruna, or crown (Kč.), which is divided into 100 haléř, or halers. There are (little-used) coins of 10, 20, and 50 halers; coins of 1, 2, 5, 10, 20, and 50 Kč., and notes of 10, 20, 50, 100, 200, 500, 1,000 Kč, and 5,000 Kč. The 100-Kč. notes are by far the most useful. The 1,000-Kč. note may not always be accepted for small purchases, because the proprietor may not have enough change.

Try to avoid exchanging money at hotels or private exchange booths, including the ubiquitous Čekobanka and Exact Change booths. They routinely take commissions of 8%–10%. The best place to exchange is at bank counters, where the commissions average 1%–3%. Although the crown is more or less convertible, you will still encounter difficulty in exchanging your money when you leave. To facilitate this process, keep your original exchange receipts so no one will think you bought your crowns on the black market. It is technically illegal to buy crowns abroad and bring them into the Czech Republic (or to take them out when you leave), although this is not strictly controlled. The black market for Western currencies is still thriving, but it's best to keep well away; such deals are strictly illegal and if caught, you risk deportation. At press time (summer 1994) the official exchange rate was around 30 Kč. to the U.S. dollar and 43 Kč. to the pound sterling. There is no longer a special exchange rate for tourists.

What It Will Cost

Despite rising inflation, the Czech Republic is still generally a bargain by Western standards. Prague remains the exception, however. Hotel prices, in particular, frequently meet or exceed the average for the U.S. and Western European—and are higher than the standard of facilities would warrant. Nevertheless, you can still find bargain private accommodations. The prices at tourist resorts outside of the capital are lower and, in the outlying areas and off the beaten track, incredibly low. Tourists can now legally pay for hotel rooms in crowns, although some hotels still insist on payment in "hard" (i.e., Western) currency.

Sample Costs A cup of coffee will cost about 15 Kč.; museum entrance, 20 Kč.; a good theater seat, up to 100 Kč.; a cinema seat, 30 Kč.; ½ liter (pint) of beer, 15 Kč.; a 1-mile taxi ride, 60 Kč.; a bottle of Moravian wine in a good restaurant, 100 Kč-150 Kč.; a glass (2 deciliters or 7 ounces) of wine, 25 Kč.

Passports and Visas

If your passport is lost or stolen abroad, report the loss immediately to the nearest embassy or consulate and to the local police. If you can provide the consular officer with the information contained in the passport, you will generally be issued a new passport promptly. For this reason, it is a good idea to keep a photocopy of the data page of your passport separate from your money and traveler's checks. You should also leave a photocopy with a relative or friend at home.

U.S. Citizens All U.S. citizens, even infants, need a valid passport to enter the Czech Republic and Slovakia for stays of up to 30 days. No visa is required to enter these countries.

You can pick up new and renewal passport application forms at any of the 13 U.S. Passport Agency offices and at some post offices and courthouses. Although passports are usually mailed within four weeks of the receipt of your application, allow five weeks or more from April through summer. Call the Department of State Office of Passport Services' information line (tel. 202/647–0518) for fees, documentation requirements, and other details.

Canadian Citizens Canadian citizens are required to have a passport and a visa for stays of up to 30 days. To obtain a visa, you must have a valid passport, one passport-type photo, a completed application, and the C$50 fee. For applications and further information, contact the Czech Republic Embassy (541 Sussex Dr., Ottawa, Ont. K1N 6Z6, tel. 613/562–3875).

U.K. Citizens Citizens of the United Kingdom need a valid passport to enter the Czech Republic and Slovakia (cost £18 for a standard 32-page passport). A British Visitors Passport is not acceptable. Visas are not required.

Customs and Duties

On Arrival You may import duty-free into the Czech Republic 250 cigarettes or the equivalent in tobacco, 1 liter of spirits, 2 liters of wine, and ½ liter of perfume. You may also bring up to 1,000 Kč. worth of gifts and souvenirs.

If you take into the Czech Republic any valuables or foreign-made equipment from home, such as cameras, it's wise to carry the original receipts with you or register the items with U.S. Customs before you leave (Form 4457). Otherwise you could end up paying duty upon your return.

Returning If you've been out of the country for at least 48
Home hours and haven't already used the exemption,
U.S. Customs or any part of it, in the past 30 days, you may bring home $400 worth of foreign goods duty-free. So can each member of your family, regardless of age; and your exemptions may be pooled, so one of you can bring in more if another brings in less. A flat 10% duty applies to the next $1,000 of goods; above $1,400, the rate varies with the merchandise. (If the 48-hour or 30-day limits apply, your duty-free allowance drops to $25, which may not be pooled.) Please note that these are the *general* rules, applicable to most countries; more generous allowances for *some* items, including arts and handicrafts, are in effect for the Czech Republic. On the other hand, crystal and some other items not bought at hard-currency shops may be subject to hefty taxes. Only antiques bought at Tuzex or specially appointed shops may be exported.

Travelers 21 or older may bring back 1 liter of alcohol duty-free, provided the beverage laws of the state through which they reenter the United States allow it. In addition, 100 non-Cuban cigars and 200 cigarettes are allowed, regardless of your age. Antiques and works of art more than 100 years old are duty-free.

Gifts valued at less than $50 may be mailed to the United States duty-free, with a limit of one package per day per addressee, and do not count as part of your exemption (do not send alcohol or tobacco products or perfume valued at more than $5); mark the package "Unsolicited Gift" and write the nature of the gift and its retail value on the outside. Most reputable stores will handle the mailing for you.

For a copy of "Know Before You Go," a free brochure detailing what you may and may not bring back to the United States, rates of duty, and other pointers, contact the **U.S. Customs Service** (Box 7407, Washington, DC 20044, tel. 202/927–6724). A copy of "GSP and the Traveler" is available from the same source.

Canadian Customs Once per calendar year, when you've been out of Canada for at least seven days, you may bring in C$300 worth of goods duty-free. If you've been away less than seven days but more than 48 hours, the duty-free exemption drops to C$100 but can be claimed any number of times (as can a C$20 duty-free exemption for absences of 24 hours or more). You cannot combine the yearly and 48-hour exemptions, use the C$300 exemption only partially (to save the balance for a later trip), or pool exemptions with family members. Goods claimed under the C$300 exemption may follow you by mail; those claimed under the lesser exemptions must accompany you upon your return.

Alcohol and tobacco products may be included in the yearly and 48-hour exemptions but not in the 24-hour exemption. If you meet the age requirements of the province through which you reenter Canada, you may bring in, duty-free, 1.14 liters (40 imperial ounces) of wine or liquor *or* two dozen 12-ounce cans or bottles of beer or ale. If you are 16 or older, you may bring in, duty-free, 200 cigarettes, 50 cigars or cigarillos, and 400 tobacco sticks or 400 grams of manufactured tobacco.

An unlimited number of gifts valued up to C$60 each may be mailed to Canada duty-free. These do not count as part of your exemption. Label the package "Unsolicited Gift—Value under $60." Alcohol and tobacco are excluded.

For more information, including details of duties on items that exceed your duty-free limit, ask the Revenue Canada Customs and Excise and Taxation Department (2265 St. Laurent Blvd. S. Ottawa, Ont., K1G 4K3, tel. 613/957–0275) for a copy of the free brochure "I Declare/Je Déclare."

U.K. Customs From countries outside the European Community (EC), including those covered in this book, you may import, duty-free, 200 cigarettes, 100 cigarillos, 50 cigars or 250 grams of tobacco; 1 liter of spirits or 2 liters of fortified or sparkling wine; 2 liters of still table wine; 60 milliliters of perfume; 250 milliliters of toilet water; and £36 worth of other goods, including gifts and souvenirs.

For further information or a copy of "A Guide for Travellers," which details standard customs procedures as well as what you may bring into the United Kingdom from abroad, contact HM Customs and Excise (Dorset House, Stamford St., London SE1 9PY, tel. 0171/928–3344).

Arriving and Departing

From North America by Plane

Flights are either nonstop, direct, or connecting. A **nonstop** flight requires no change of plane and makes no stops. A **direct** flight stops at least once and can involve a change of plane, although the flight number remains the same; if the first leg is late, the second waits. This is not the case with a **connecting** flight, which involves a different plane and a different flight number.

Airports and Airlines All international flights to the Czech Republic fly into Prague's **Ruzyně Airport,** about 20 kilometers (12 miles) northwest of downtown. The airport is small and easy to negotiate.

ČSA, (Czechoslovak Airlines), the Czech and Slovak national carrier (tel. 718/656–8439), maintains regular direct flights to Prague from New York's JFK Airport, and twice-weekly flights from Chicago, Los Angeles, and Montreal.

Major airlines that serve Prague include **Air France** (tel. 02/2422–7164), **Alitalia** (tel. 02/2481–0079), **Austrian Airlines** (tel. 02/231–3378), **British Airways** (tel. 02/232–9020), **ČSA** (tel. 02/2421–0132), **Delta** (tel. 02/2481–2110), **KLM** (tel. 02/2422–8678), **Lufthansa** (tel. 02/2481–1007), **SAS** (tel. 02/2421–4749), and **Swissair** (tel. 02/2481–2111).

Between the A special ČSA shuttle bus stops at all major ho-
Airport and tels. The bus departs two to three times an hour
Downtown between 7:40 AM and 9:30 PM from the bus stop directly outside the main entrance. You can buy
your ticket (cost: 60 Kč.) on the bus. Regular municipal bus service (Bus 119) connects the airport
and the **Dejvická** metro stop; the fare is 6 Kč.
From Dejvická you can take a subway to the city
center, but you must buy an additional ticket (6
Kč.). To reach Wenceslas Square, get off at the
Můstek station.

Taxis offer the easiest and most convenient way
of getting downtown. The trip is a straight shot
down the Evropská Boulevard and takes ap-
proximately 20 minutes. The road is not usually
busy, but you anticipate an additional 20 minutes during rush hour (7–9 AM and 4–7 PM). The
ride costs about 300 Kč.

Flying Time From New York, a nonstop flight to Prague
takes 9–10 hours; with a stopover, the journey
will take at least 12–13 hours. From Montreal
nonstop it is 7½ hours; from Los Angeles, 16
hours.

From the United Kingdom

By Plane **British Airways** (tel. 0171/897–4000) has daily
nonstop service to Prague from London (with
connections to major British cities); **ČSA** (tel.
0171/255–1898) flies five times a week nonstop
from London. The flight takes around three
hours.

By Car The most convenient ferry ports for Prague are
Hoek van Holland and Ostend. To reach Prague
from either ferry port, drive first to Cologne
(Köln) and then through either Dresden or
Frankfurt.

By Bus There is no direct bus service from the United
Kingdom to the Czech Republic; the closest you
can get is Munich, and from there the train is
your best bet. **International Express** (Coach
Travel Center, 13 Lower Regent St., London
SW1Y 4LR, tel. 0171/439–9368) operates daily
in summer, leaving London's Victoria Coach
Station in mid-evening and arriving in Munich
about 23 hours later.

By Train There are no direct trains from London. You can take a direct train from Paris via Frankfurt to Prague (daily) or from Berlin via Dresden to Prague (three times a day). Vienna is a good starting point for Prague, Brno, or Bratislava. There are three trains a day from Vienna's Franz Josefsbahnhof to Prague via Třeboň and Tábor (5½ hours) and two from the Südbahnhof (South Station) via Brno (five hours).

Staying in Prague

Important Addresses and Numbers

Tourist Information **Čedok,** the ubiquitous state-run travel agency, is the first stop for general tourist information and city maps. Čedok will also exchange money, arrange guided tours, and book passage on airlines, buses, and trains. You can pay for Čedok services, including booking rail tickets, with any major credit card. Note limited weekend hours. *Main office: Na příkopě 18, tel. 02/2419-7111, fax 02/232-1656. Open weekdays 8:30-5, Sat. 8:30-12:30.*

The **Prague Information Service** (PIS, Staroměstské nám. 22, tel. 02/224311, fax 02/226067) is generally less helpful than Čedok but offers city maps and general tourist information. It can also exchange money and help in obtaining tickets for cultural events.

The friendly, English-speaking staff at **AVE,** located in the main train station (Hlavní nádraží, tel. 02/2422-3226, fax 02/2422-3463), will gladly sell you a map of Prague (cost: 10 Kč.) and answer basic questions. The organization also offers an excellent room-finding service and will change money. The office is open daily 6 AM-11 PM.

Prague Suites, located at Melantrichova 8 (tel. 02/2423-0467, fax 02/2422-9363), can assist in finding luxury accommodations in private apartments; it can also help secure concert tickets and provide general tourist information.

To find out what's on for the month and to get the latest tips for shopping, dining, and entertainment, consult one or both of Prague's two

English-language newspapers, **The Prague Post** (weekly, 30 Kč.) and **Prognosis** (biweekly, 25 Kč.). Both have comprehensive entertainment listings and can be purchased at the AHC and most downtown newsstands. The monthly **Prague Guide,** available at newsstands and tourist offices for 25 Kč., provides a good overview of major cultural events and has comprehensive listings of restaurants, hotels, and organizations offering traveler assistance.

Embassies **U.S. Embassy.** Tržiště 15, Malá Strana, tel. 02/2451–0847. **British Embassy.** Thunovská ul. 14, Malá Strana, tel. 02/2451–0439. **Canadian Embassy.** Mickiewiczova ul. 6, Hradčany, tel. 02/2431–1108.

Emergencies **Police** (tel. 158). **Ambulance** (tel. 155). **Medical emergencies** tel. (02/5292–2146 or 02/5292–2191 on weekends). **Dentists** (tel. 02/2422–7663 for 24-hour emergency service).

English-Language Bookstores Part bookstore and part café, **The Globe** (Janovského 14, Prague 7, close to Vltavska metro station) carries a diverse and reasonably priced selection of used and new paperbacks. **Bohemian Ventures** (Nám. Jana Palacha, open weekdays 9–6, Sat. 9–12) at the Charles University Philosophical Faculty near Staroměstská metro station stocks mostly Penguin-published titles. Street vendors on Wenceslas Square and Na příkopě carry leading foreign newspapers and periodicals. For hiking maps and auto atlases, try **Melantrich** (Na příkopě 3, Nové Město).

Late-Night Pharmacy The pharmacy at Na příkopě 7 (tel. 02/220081), just a few steps down from Wenceslas Square, is open 24 hours.

Travel Agencies **Thomas Cook** (Václavské nám. 47, tel. 02/2422–9537, fax 02/265695) and **American Express** (Václavské nám. 56, tel. 02/2422–7786, fax 02/2422–7708) can make travel arrangements, exchange money, and issue and redeem traveler's checks. American Express maintains an automatic-teller machine for use by card members. Both agencies are open weekdays 9–6; American Express is also open Saturday 9–12.

Čedok (*see* Tourist Information, *above*) is a good source for international train and bus tickets and one of the few places in town where it is possible to use a credit card for purchasing train tickets.

Two agencies, **České Dráhy** (Na Příkopě 31, tel. 02/2422–4572) and **Wolff** (Na příkopě 22, tel. 02/2422–9957, fax 02/2422–8849), are good sources for discounted international air and bus tickets. Both are open weekdays 9–6 and Saturday 9–noon.

Telephones

Local Calls Coin-operated telephones take either just 1-Kč. coins or 1-, 2-, and 5-Kč. coins. Many newer public phones operate only with a special telephone card, available from newsstands and tobacconists in denominations of 100 Kč. and 190 Kč. A call within Prague costs 1 Kč. To make a call, lift the receiver and listen for the dial tone, a series of long buzzes. Dial the number. Public phones are located in metro stations and on street corners; unfortunately, they're often out of order. Try asking in a hotel if you're stuck.

International Calls To reach an English-speaking operator in the United States, dial tel. 00–420–00101 (AT&T) or tel. 00–420–00112 (MCI). The operator will connect your collect or credit-card call at standard AT&T or MCI rates. In Prague, the main post office (Hlavní pošta, Jindřišská ul. 14), open 24 hours, is the best place to make direct-dial long-distance calls. Otherwise, ask the receptionist at any hotel to put a call through for you, though beware: The more expensive the hotel, the more expensive the call will be.

Mail

Postal Rates Postcards to the United States cost 6 Kč.; letters, 11 Kč.; to Great Britain a postcard is 4 Kč.; a letter, 6 Kč. Prices are due for an increase in 1995, so check with your hotel for current rates. You can buy stamps at post offices, hotels, and shops that sell postcards.

Receiving Mail If you don't know where you'll be staying, **American Express** mail service is a great convenience, available at no charge to anyone holding an American Express credit card or carrying American Express traveler's checks. The

American Express office is located on Wenceslas Square in central Prague. You can also have mail held *poste restante* (general delivery) at post offices in major towns, but the letters should be marked *Pošta 1* to designate the city's main post office. The poste restante window is No. 28 at the main post office in Prague (Jindřišská ul. 14). You will be asked for identification when you collect your mail.

Getting Around Prague

To see Prague properly, there is no alternative to walking, especially since much of the city center is off limits to automobiles. And the walking couldn't be more pleasant—most of it along the beautiful bridges and cobblestone streets of the city's historic core. Before venturing out, however, be sure you have a good map.

By Subway Prague's subway system, the metro, is clean and reliable. Trains run every day from 5 AM to midnight. *Jízdenky* (tickets) cost 6 Kč. apiece and can be bought at hotels, tobacconists, or at vending machines at station entrances. Have some small coins handy for the machines. Validate the tickets yourself at machines before descending the escalators; each ticket is good for 60 minutes of uninterrupted travel. Special daily and extended passes, valid for all buses, trams, and subways, can be purchased at newsstands, train stations, and Čedok offices. A one-day pass costs 50 Kč., a two-day pass 85 Kč., a three-day pass 110 Kč., and a five-day pass 170 Kč. Trains are patrolled frequently; the fine for riding without a valid ticket is 200 Kč.

By Bus and Tram Prague's extensive bus and streetcar network allows for fast, efficient travel throughout the city. Tickets are the same as those used for the metro (cost: 6 Kč.), although you validate them at machines inside the bus or streetcar. Bus and tram tickets are valid only for a particular ride; if you change to a different tram or bus, or get on the metro, you must validate a new ticket. Signal to stop the bus by pushing the button by the doors. Tram doors open automatically at all scheduled stops. Special "night trams" run every night from around midnight to 5 AM and connect the city center with outlying areas.

By Taxi Dishonest taxi drivers are the shame of the nation. Luckily visitors do not need to rely on taxis for trips within the city center (it's usually easier to walk or take the subway). Typical scams include drivers doctoring the meter or simply failing to turn the meter on and then demanding an exorbitant sum at the end of the ride. In an honest cab, the meter will start at 10 Kč. and increase by 12 Kč. per kilometer (½-mile) or 1 Kč. per minute at rest. Most rides within town should cost no more than 80 Kč.–100 Kč. To minimize the chances of getting ripped off, avoid taxi stands in Wenceslas Square and other heavily touristed areas. The best alternative is to phone for a taxi in advance. Some reputable firms are **AAA Taxi** (tel. 02/342410), **BM Taxi** (tel. 02/256144), and **Sedop** (tel. 02/725110). Many firms have English-speaking operators.

Guided Tours

Čedok's (tel. 02/231–8949) three-hour "Historical Prague" tour (450 Kč.), offered year-round, is a combination bus-walking venture that covers all of the major sights. It departs daily at 10 AM from the Čedok office at Bilkova ulice 21 (near the InterContinental Hotel). Between May and September, "Panoramic Prague" (290 Kč.), an abbreviated version of the above tour, departs daily except Sunday at 11 AM and 4 PM from the Čedok office at Na příkopé 18. On Monday and Thursday Čedok also offers "Old Prague on Foot," a slower-paced, four-hour walking tour that departs at 9 AM from Na příkopé 18. The price is 290 Kč.

Many private firms now offer combination bus-walking tours of the city that typically last two or three hours and cost 300 Kč.–400 Kč. For more information, address inquiries to any of the dozen operators with booths on Staroměstské nám (near the Jan Hus monument) or Náměstí Republiky (near the Obecní Dům).

Personal You can contact the Čedok office at Bilkova 6
Guides (tel. 02/231–8949) to arrange a personalized walking tour. Times and itineraries are negotiable; prices start at around 350 Kč. per hour.

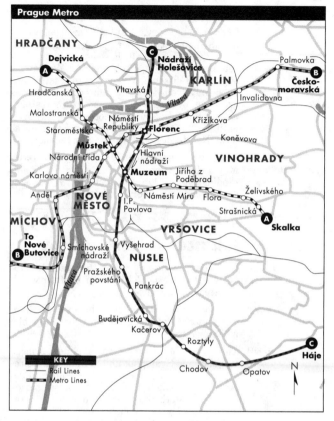

Prague Metro

HRADČANY

Dejvická

Hradčanská

Malostranská

Staroměstská

Náměstí
Republiky

Müstek

Národní třída

Karlovo náměstí

Anděl

NOVÉ
MĚSTO

MÍCHOV

To
Nové
Butovice

Smíchovské
nádraží

Vltava

Pražského
povstání

Pankrác

Budějovická

Kačerov

Roztyly

Chodov

Opatov

Háje

Vltavská

Vltava

Florenc

Hlavní
nádraží

Muzeum

I.P.
Pavlova

Vyšehrad

NUSLE

Nádraží
Holešovice

KARLÍN

Palmovka

Česko-
moravská

Invalidovna

Křižíkova

Koněvova

VINOHRADY

Jiřího z
Poděbrad

Náměstí Míru

Flora

Želivského

Strašnická

Skalka

VRŠOVICE

KEY
— Rail Lines
▪▪▪ Metro Lines

N

Opening and Closing Times

Though hours vary, most banks are open weekdays 8–3:30, with an hour's lunch break. Private exchange offices usually have longer hours. Museums are usually open daily except Monday (or Tuesday) 9–5; some, including many castles, are open only from May through October. Stores are open weekdays 9–6; some grocery stores open at 6 AM. Department stores often stay open until 7 PM. On Saturday, most stores close at noon. Nearly all stores are closed on Sunday.

National Holidays   January 1; Easter Monday; May 1 (Labor Day); May 9 (Liberation); July 5 (Sts. Cyril and Methodius); July 6 (Jan Hus); October 28 (Independence); and December 24, 25, and 26.

The Czech Republic at a Glance: A Chronology

c 400 BC   Bohemia, the main region of the Czech Republic, is settled by the Celtic Boii tribe, from which the area gets its name.

c 500   Closely related Slavic tribes begin to settle in the regions that make up the Czech Republic and Slovakia.

846–894   The great Moravian Empire under princes Ratislav and Svätopluk unites Bohemia, Moravia, and most of Slovakia, and extends into Poland and Hungary. Byzantine missionaries Cyril and Methodius—credited with the creation of the Cyrillic alphabet—translate Christian liturgy into Slavonic and convert much of the region.

892   German king Arnulf asks the help of the Magyars to fight Moravia. The Magyars destroy the Moravian Empire by 907 and settle in the region of modern Hungary.

907   Slovakia is conquered by the Magyars, beginning a thousand years of subjugation by Hungary.

1029   Czech princes aligned with the Holy Roman Empire shift the center of power from Moravia to Bohemia. Moravia is annexed by Bohemia.

1348 Charles University, the first university in Central Europe, is built in Prague.

1355 Czech prince Charles IV, known as the "Father of the country," is named Holy Roman Emperor. Prague becomes a cultural center of Europe as well as capital of the empire.

1415 Czech religious reformer Jan Hus is burned at the stake, but the Czech Reformation, or Hussite movement, continues.

1526 Ferdinand I of Habsburg inherits the crown of Bohemia. Habsburgs rule the Czech region, with few brief interruptions, until 1918. Ottoman Turks destroy the Hungarian army at Mohacs. The Ottoman Empire gradually takes control of all but the westernmost region of Hungary.

1848 Bohemia attempts to establish an autonomous government; many of its demands are met by the emperor in April. Hapsburg emperor Ferdinand I abdicates in favor of his 18-year-old nephew Franz Josef, whose iron rule continues until 1916. Romania, with Austria's support, begins warfare against Hungary.

1914 Archduke Ferdinand, a strong supporter of the rights of Transylvania's Romanians, is assassinated by a Bosnian Serb. Hungary and Bulgaria fight with the Central Powers—Austria and Germany—in World War I.

1916 The Kingdom of Poland is reestablished by Germany and Austria in the hope of gaining Polish support in the war, but little support for the puppet kingdom materializes. Death of Franz Josef.

1918 In President Woodrow Wilson's "14 points" speech, the 10th point demands autonomy for the peoples of Austria-Hungary. The Republic of Czechoslovakia is formed; Tomaš Garrigue Masaryk, who led the independence movement, is named its first president.

1920 The Versailles settlement forces Hungary to give up huge areas of territory, and more than half of its prewar population. Czechoslovakia receives Slovakia and Ruthenia. Czechoslovakia adopts its first democratic constitution and national elections are held.

1938 The Munich Pact formed by Germany, Italy, Britain, and France allows Hitler to annex the German-Czech border area known as Sudetenland.

1939 Slovakia led by Catholic priest Father Josef Tiso declares its independence. Two days later Slovakia becomes a protectorate of Nazi Germany and remains a semi-independent state throughout the war. Seventy thousand out of 95,000 Slovak Jews are exterminated by the end of the war. Bohemia and Moravia are proclaimed protectorates of Nazi Germany.

1945 Prague is liberated by the Soviet army, giving the Soviet Union an important political victory in Czechoslovakia.

1946 The Czechoslovak Communist party wins its first postwar national elections but does not receive a majority.

1968 After several years of demands for political liberalization, Slovak political reformer Alexander Dubček is named the first secretary of the Czech Communist party, ushering in the Prague Spring. Dubček tries to create "socialism with a human face," calling for multiparty democratic elections. In August, Soviet and other Warsaw Pact troops invade Czechoslovakia.

1969 Czech student Jan Palach sets himself on fire to protest the forced ending of the Prague Spring; Palach's martyrdom becomes an important source of motivation for the revolution of 1989.

1977 Czech intellectuals, including playwright Václav Havel, sign Charter 77, a declaration of grievances with the hard-line communist government.

1978 Karol Wojtyła, the Cardinal of Kraków, is elected Pope John Paul II.

1989 Demonstrations in Prague in honor of the 20th anniversary of the death of Jan Palach lead to sweeping political and economic reforms, including free elections. Czech police beat protesters at a rally in Prague and at least one student is reportedly killed. This proves to be the catalyst for the most rapid revolution in Eastern Europe. Two days later the organization Civic Forum is created by Václav Havel and others. A day after that, 200,000 people pack Wenceslas Square and demand democracy. On November 24, Alexander Dubček returns to Prague for his first public appearance there since 1969 and addresses a mass demonstration. The Communist party relinquishes its "leading role" on November 29. Václav Havel replaces Husák as president on December 29. Dubček is named speaker of the national Parliament.

1990   Under pressure from Slovak nationalists, Czechoslovakia changes its name to the Czech and Slovak Federative Republic. Czechoslovakia holds its first free democratic elections since 1946. Civic Forum and its counterpart in Slovakia, Public Against Violence, win convincingly in races against as many as 21 parties. Václav Havel is elected to a second two-year term as president of Czechoslovakia. President Bush is the first American president to visit Prague.

1991   Czechoslovakia sends 200 troops to the Gulf War, signaling its support of the Western cause. The Czech Civic Forum party splits into free-market and social-democratic factions, while the leading Slovak party, Public Against Violence, splits along pro- and antiseparatist lines.

1992   Parliamentary elections in Czechoslovakia lead to a deeper split between the Czech and Slovak republics. Newly elected Czech premier Václav Klaus and Slovak nationalist leader Vladimir Mečiar fail to agree on terms for a common government and direct their respective parliaments to develop guidelines for the establishment of separate governments. Unwilling to preside over the dissolution of the nation, Václav Havel resigns the presidency in July.

1993   Failing to find a compromise, Czech and Slovak leaders split the 74-year-old Czechoslovak federation on Jan. 1, 1993. The Czech Republic and Slovakia become fully sovereign and separate countries. Václav Havel is elected by Parliament to be the new Czech president; the Slovaks appoint former banker Michael Kováč.

2 Exploring Prague

Prague originally comprised five independent towns, represented today by its main historical districts: **Hradčany** (Castle Area), **Malá Strana** (Little Quarter), **Staré Město** (Old Town), **Nové Město** (New Town), and **Josefov** (the Jewish Quarter). The spine of the city is the river Vltava (Moldau), which runs from south to north with a single sharp curve to the east.

Hradčany, the seat of Czech royalty for hundreds of years, has as its center the **Pražský Hrad** (Prague Castle), which overlooks the city from its hilltop west of the Vltava. Steps lead down from Hradčany to Malá Strana, an area dense with ornate mansions built by 17th- and 18th-century nobility.

Karlův Most (Charles Bridge) connects Malá Strana with Staré Město. Just a few blocks east of the bridge is the focal point of the Old Town, **Staroměstské náměstí** (Old Town Square). Staré Město is bounded by the curving Vltava and three large commercial avenues: **Revoluční** to the east, **Na příkopě** to the southeast, and **Národní třída** to the south.

Beyond lies the Nové Město; several blocks south is **Karlovo náměstí**, the city's largest square. Roughly 1 kilometer (½ mile) farther south is **Vyšehrad,** an ancient castle site high above the river.

On a promontory to the east of Wenceslas Square stretches **Vinohrady,** once the favored neighborhood of well-to-do Czechs; below Vinohrady lie the crumbling neighborhoods of **Žižkov** to the north and **Nusle** to the south. On the west banks of the Vltava south and east of Hradčany lie many older residential neighborhoods and enormous parks. About 3 kilometers (2 miles) from the center in every direction, communist-era housing projects begin their unappealing sprawl.

Highlights for First-Time Visitors

Charles Bridge (*see* Tour 3)
Old Town Square (*see* Tour 1)
Prague Castle (*see* Tour 5)
St. Nicholas Church (Chram sv. Mikuláše) in Malá Strana (*see* Tour 3)

Týn Church (*see* Tour 1)

Tour 1: Staré Město

Numbers in the margin correspond to points of interest on the Prague (Tours 1–4) map.

❶ **Václavské náměstí** (Wenceslas Square), convenient to hotels and transportation, is an appropriate place to begin a tour of Staré Město (Old Town). A long, gently sloping boulevard rather than a square in the usual sense, Václavské náměstí is bordered at the top (the southern end) by the Czech National Museum and at the bottom by the pedestrian shopping areas of **Národní třída** and **Na příkopě.** Visitors may recognize this spot from their television sets, for it was here that some 500,000 students and citizens gathered in the heady days of November 1989 to protest the policies of the former communist regime. The government capitulated after a week of demonstrations, without a shot fired or the loss of a single life, bringing to power the first democratic government in 40 years (under playwright-president Václav Havel). Today this peaceful transfer of power is proudly referred to as the "Velvet" or "Gentle" Revolution (*něžná revolucia*).

It was only fitting that the 1989 revolution should take place on Wenceslas Square. Throughout much of Czech history, the square has served as the focal point for popular discontent. In 1848 citizens protested Habsburg rule ❷ at the **statue of St. Wenceslas** in front of the National Museum. In 1939 residents gathered to oppose Hitler's takeover of Bohemia and Moravia. It was here also, in 1969, that the student Jan Palach set himself on fire to protest the bloody invasion of his country by the Soviet Union and other Warsaw Pact countries in August of the previous year. The invasion ended the "Prague Spring," a cultural and political movement emphasizing free expression that was supported by Alexander Dubček, the popular leader at the time. Although Dubček never intended to dismantle communist authority completely, his political and economic reforms proved too daring for fellow comrades in the rest of Eastern Europe. In the months following the invasion, conservatives loyal to the Soviet Union were installed in all influential positions. The subsequent two decades ushered in a period of cultural stagnation. Thousands of residents left the country or went underground; many more resigned themselves to lives of minimal expectations and small pleasures.

Today Wenceslas Square offers Prague's liveliest street scene. Don't miss the dense maze of arcades tucked away from the street in buildings that line both sides. You'll find an odd assortment of cafés, discos, ice cream parlors, and movie houses, all seemingly unfazed by the passage of time. At night the square changes character somewhat as dance music pours out from the crowded discos and leather-jacketed cronies crowd around the taxi stands.

Although Wenceslas Square was first laid out by Charles IV in 1348 as the center of Nové Město (New Town), few buildings of architectural merit line the square today. Even the imposing ❸ structure of the **Národní muzeum** (Czech National Museum), designed by Prague architect Josef Schulz and built between 1885 and 1890, does not really come into its own until it is bathed in nighttime lighting. During the day, the grandiose edifice seems an inappropriate venue for a musty collection of stones and bones, minerals, and coins. This museum is only for dedicated fans of the genre! *Václavské nám. 68, tel. 02/2423–0485. Admission: 20 Kč. Open Wed.–Mon. 9–5.*

❹ One eye-catching building on the square is the **Hotel Europa** at No. 25, a riot of Art Nouveau that recalls the glamorous world of turn-of-the-century Prague. Don't miss the elegant stained glass and mosaics of the café and restaurant. The terrace, serving drinks in the summer, is an excellent spot for people-watching.

To begin the approach to the Old Town proper, walk past the tall, Art Deco, Koruna complex (once an enormous fast-food joint, now an office complex) and turn onto the handsome pedestrian zone called **Na příkopě**. The name means "at the moat," harking back to the time when the street was indeed a moat separating Staré Město on the left from Nové Město on the right.

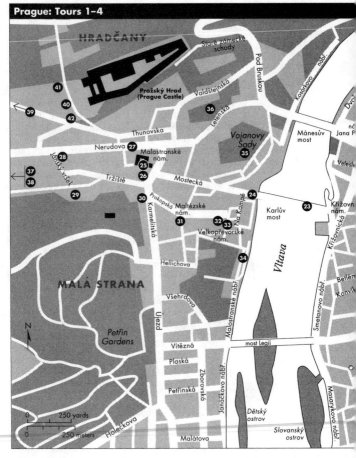

Prague: Tours 1–4

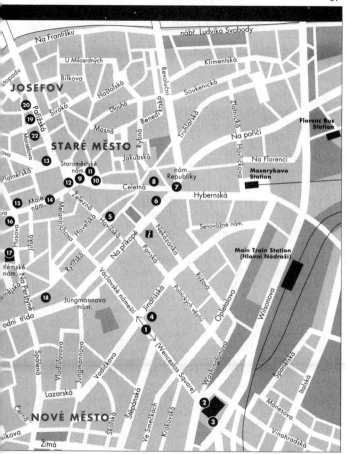

Today Na příkopě is prime shopping territory, its smaller boutiques considered far more elegant than the motley collection of stores on Wenceslas Square. But don't expect much real elegance here: After 40 years of communist orthodoxy in the fashion world, it will be many years before the boutiques really can match Western European standards.

❺ Turn left onto Havířská ulice and follow this small alley to the glittering green-and-cream splendor of the newly renovated **Stavovské divadlo** (Estates Theater). Built in the 1780s in the classical style and reopened in 1991 after years of renovation, the handsome theater was for many years a beacon of Czech-language culture in a city long dominated by German. It is probably best known as the site of the world premiere of Mozart's opera *Don Giovanni* in October 1787, with the composer himself in the conducting role. Prague audiences were quick to acknowledge Mozart's genius. The opera was an instant hit here, though it flopped nearly everywhere else in Europe. Mozart wrote most of the opera's second act in Prague at the Villa Bertramka, where he was a frequent guest (*see* Off the Beaten Track, *below*).

❻ Return to Na příkopě, turn left, and continue to the end of the street. On weekdays between 8 AM and 5 PM, it's well worth taking a peek at the stunning interior of the **Živnostenská banka** (Merchants' Bank) at No. 20. The style, a tasteful example of 19th-century exuberance, reflected the city's growing prosperity at the time. Ignore the guards and walk up the decorated stairs to the beautiful main banking room (note, however, that taking photos is forbidden).

❼ Na příkopě ends abruptly at the **Náměstí republiky** (Republic Square), an important transportation hub (with a metro stop) but a square that has never really come together as a vital public space, perhaps because of its jarring architectural eclecticism. Taken one by one, each building is interesting in its own right, but the ensemble is less than the sum of the parts. The severe Depression-era facade of the **Česká národní banka** (Czech National Bank, Na pří-

kopě 30) makes the building look more like a for-
tress than the nation's central bank.

Close by stands the stately **Prašná brána** (Powder Tower), its festive Gothic spires looming
above the square. Construction of the tower,
one of the city's 13 original gates, was begun by
King Vladislav II of Jagiello in 1475. At the
time, the kings of Bohemia maintained their
royal residence next door (on the site of the current Obecní dům, the Municipal House), and the
tower was intended to be the grandest gate of
all. But Vladislav was Polish and thus heartily
disliked by the rebellious Czech citizens of
Prague. Nine years after he assumed power,
fearing for his life, he moved the royal court
across the river to Prague Castle. Work on the
tower was abandoned and the half-finished
structure was used to store gunpowder—hence
its odd name—until the end of the 17th century.
The oldest part of the tower is the base; the gold-
en spires were not added until the end of the last
century. The climb to the top affords a striking
view of the Old Town and Prague Castle in the
distance. *Nám. Republiky. Admission: 20 Kč.
adults, 10 Kč. students. Open Apr.–Oct., daily
9–6.*

Adjacent to the dignified Powder Tower, the
Obecní dům (Municipal House) looks decidedly
decadent. The style, mature Art Nouveau, recalls the lengths the Czech middle classes went
to at the turn of the century to imitate Paris,
then the epitome of style and glamour. Much of
the interior bears the work of the Art Nouveau
master Alfons Mucha and other leading Czech
artists. Mucha decorated the main Hall of the
Lord Mayor upstairs. His magical frescoes depicting Czech history are considered a master-
piece of the genre. Throughout the year some of
the city's best concerts are held in its beautiful
Smetana Hall, on the second floor.

Time Out The **Obecní Dům café**, usually packed with tourists, serves good coffee and cake in a resplen-
dent setting. Ignore the slow service and enjoy
the view. If you prefer a subtler elegance, head
around the corner to the café at **Hotel Paříž** (U

Obecního domu 1), a Jugendstil jewel tucked
away on a quiet street.

Walk through the arch at the base of the Powder
Tower and down the formal **Celetná ulice,** the
first leg of the so-called Royal Way, in years past
the traditional coronation route of the Czech
kings. Monarchs favored this route primarily
for its stunning entry into **Staroměstské náměstí**
(Old Town Square) and because the houses along
Celetná were among the city's finest, providing
a suitable backdrop to the coronation proces-
sion. (Most of the facades indicate that the
buildings are from the 17th or 18th century, but
appearances are deceiving: Many of the houses
in fact have foundations dating from the 12th
❽ century or earlier.) The pink **Sixt House** at
Celetná 2 sports one of the street's most handsome, if restrained, Baroque facades. The house
itself dates from the 12th century—its Romanesque vaults are still visible in the wine restaurant in the basement.

❾ **Staroměstské náměstí** (Old Town Square), at the
end of Celetná, is dazzling (the scaffolding that
obscured many of its finest buildings during recent renovations is finally down). Long the
heart of the Old Town, the square grew to its
present proportions when the city's original
marketplace was moved away from the river in
the 12th century. Its shape and appearance have
changed little over the years. During the day
the square takes on a festive atmosphere as musicians vie for the favor of onlookers, hefty
young men in medieval outfits mint coins, and
artists display their renditions of Prague street
scenes. It's worth coming back to the square at
night, as well, when the unlit shadowy towers of
the Týn Church (to your right as you enter the
square) rise forebodingly over the glowing Baroque facades. The crowds thin out, and the
ghosts of the square's stormy past return.

During the 15th century the square was the focal point of conflict between Czech Hussites and
German Catholics. In 1422 the radical Hussite
preacher Jan Želivský was executed here for his
part in storming the New Town's town hall.
Three Catholic consuls and seven German citizens were thrown out of the window in the ensu-

ing fray—the first of Prague's many famous "defenestrations." Within a few years, the Hussites had taken over the town, expelled the Germans, and set up their own administration.

The center of their activity was the double-spired **Kostel Panny Marie před Týnem** (the Týn Church), which rises over the square from behind a row of patrician houses. Construction of its twin jet-black spires, which still jar the eye, was begun by King Jiří of Poděbrad in 1461 during the heyday of the Hussites. Jiří had a gilded chalice, the symbol of the Hussites, proudly displayed on the front gable between the two towers. Following the defeat of the Hussites by the Catholic Habsburgs, the chalice was removed and eventually replaced by a Madonna. As a final blow, the chalice was melted down and made into the Madonna's glimmering halo (you still can see it by walking into the center of the square and looking up between the spires). The entrance to the Týn Church is through the arcades, under the house at No. 604. *Celetná 5. Admission: 20 Kč. Open weekdays 9–6, Sat. 9–noon, Sun. 1–6.*

Although the exterior of the Týn Church is one of the best examples of Prague Gothic (in part the work of Peter Parler, architect of the Charles Bridge and St. Vitus Cathedral), much of the interior, including the tall nave, was rebuilt in the Baroque style in the 17th century. Some Gothic pieces remain, however: Look to the left of the main altar for a beautifully preserved set of early Gothic carvings. The main altar itself was painted by Karel Škréta, a luminary of the Czech Baroque. Before leaving the church, look for the grave marker (tucked away to the right of the main altar) of the great Danish astronomer Tycho de Brahe, who came to Prague as "Imperial Mathematicus" in 1599 under Rudolf II. As a scientist, Tycho had a place in history that is assured: Johannes Kepler (another resident of the Prague court) used Tycho's observations to formulate his laws of planetary motion. But it is myth that has endeared Tycho to the hearts of Prague residents: The robust Dane, who was apparently fond of duels, lost part of his nose in one (take a closer look at the marker). He quickly had a wax nose fashioned for everyday use but preferred to parade around on holidays and festive occasions sporting a bright silver one.

To the immediate left of the Týn Church is U Zvonů (No. 13), a Baroque structure that has been stripped down to its original Gothic elements. It occasionally hosts concerts and art exhibitions. The exhibitions change frequently, and it's worth stopping by to see what's on.

A short walk away stands the dazzling pink-and-ocher Palác Kinských (Kinský Palace), built in 1765 and considered one of Prague's finest late-Baroque structures. With its exaggerated pink overlay and numerous statues, the facade looks extreme when contrasted with the more staid Baroque elements of other nearby buildings. The palace once housed a German school (where Franz Kafka was a student for nine misery-laden years) and presently contains the National Gallery's graphics collection. The main exhibition room is on the second floor; exhibits change every few months and are usually worth seeing. It was from this building that communist leader Klement Gottwald, flanked by his comrade Clementis, first addressed the crowds after seizing power in February 1948—an event recounted in the first chapter of Milan Kundera's novel *The Book of Laughter and Forgetting*. *Staroměstské nám. 12. Admission: 10 Kč. adults, 5 Kč. children and students. Open Tues.–Sun. 10–6.*

⓫ At this end of the square, you can't help noticing the expressive Jan Hus monument. Few memorials have elicited as much controversy as this one, which was dedicated in July 1915, exactly 500 years after Hus was burned at the stake in Konstanz, Germany. Some maintain that the monument's Secessionist style (the inscription seems to come right from turn-of-the-century Vienna) clashes with the Gothic and Baroque of the square. Others dispute the romantic depiction of Hus, who appears here in flowing garb as tall and bearded. The real Hus, historians maintain, was short and had a baby face. Still, no one can take issue with the influence of this fiery preacher, whose ability to transform doctrinal disputes, both literally and metaphorically, into the language of the common man made him into a religious and national symbol for the Czechs.

Opposite the Týn Church is the Gothic
⓬ Staroměstská radnice (Old Town Hall), which gives the square its sense of importance. As you walk toward the building from the Hus monument, look for the 27 white crosses on the ground just in front of the Town Hall. These mark the spot where 27 Bohemian noblemen were killed by the Habsburgs in 1621 during the dark days following the defeat of the Czechs at the Battle of White Mountain. The grotesque spectacle, designed to quash any further national or religious opposition, took some five hours to complete, as the men were put to the sword or hanged, one by one.

The Town Hall has served as the center of administration for the Old Town since 1338, when King Johann of Luxembourg first granted the city council the right to a permanent location. Walk around the structure to the left and you'll see that it's actually a series of houses jutting into the square; they were purchased over the years and successively added to the complex. The most interesting is the **U Minuty,** the corner building to the left of the clock tower, with its 16th-century Renaissance sgraffiti of biblical and classical motifs.

The impressive 200-foot **Town Hall tower** was first built in the 14th century and given its current late-Gothic appearance around 1500 by the master Matyáš Rejsek. For a rare view of the Old Town and its maze of crooked streets and alleyways, climb to the top of the tower. The climb is not strenuous, but steep stairs at the top unfortunately prevent the disabled from enjoying the view. Enter through the door to the left of the tower.

As the hour approaches, join the crowds milling below the tower's 15th-century **Astronomical Clock** for a brief but spooky spectacle taken straight from the Middle Ages. Just before the hour, look to the upper part of the clock, where a skeleton begins by tolling a death knell and turning an hour-glass upside down. The 12 apostles parade momentarily, and then a cockerel flaps its wings and crows, piercing the air as the hour finally strikes, solemnly. To the right of the skeleton, the dreaded Turk nods his head, seemingly hinting at another invasion like those of the 16th and 17th centuries. Immediately after the hour, guided tours in English and German (German only during winter) of the Town Hall depart inside from the main desk. However, the only notables inside are the fine Renaissance ceilings and Gothic Council Room. *Staroměstské nám. Admission to hall: 20 Kč. adults, 10 Kč. children and students; admission to tower: 10 Kč. adults, 5 Kč. children and students. Hall open daily 9–6; tower open daily 10–6.*

Time Out   Staroměstské náměstí is a convenient spot for refreshments. **Tchibo,** at No. 6, has tasty sandwiches and excellent coffee, and an outdoor terrace in season.

---

⑬   Walk north along the edge of the small park beside the Town Hall to reach the Baroque **Kostel svatého Mikuláše** (Church of St. Nicholas), not to be confused with the Little Quarter's St. Nicholas Church, on the other side of the river (*see* Tour 3, *below*). Though both churches were designed in the 18th century by Prague's own master of the late Baroque, Kilian Ignaz Dientzenhofer, this St. Nicholas is probably less successful than its namesake across town in capturing the style's lyric exuberance. Still, Dientzenhofer utilized the limited space to create a structure that neither dominates nor retreats from the imposing square. The interior is compact, with a beautiful but small chandelier and an enormous black organ that seems to overwhelm the rear of the church. The church often hosts afternoon concerts.

Franz Kafka's birthplace is just to the left of St. Nicholas on U radnice. A small plaque can be found on the side of the house. For years this memorial to Kafka's birth (July 3, 1883) was the only public acknowledgment of the writer's stature in world literature, reflecting the traditionally ambiguous attitude of the Czech government to his work. The Communists were always too uncomfortable with Kafka's themes of bureaucracy and alienation to sing his praises too loudly, if at all. As a German and a Jew, moreover, Kafka could easily be dismissed as standing outside of the mainstream of Czech literature. Following the 1989 revolution, however, Kafka's popularity soared, and his works are now widely available in Czech. A fascinating little museum has been set up in the house of his birth. *U radnice 5. Admission: 20 Kč. Open daily 10–7.*

Go back to the southwest corner of Staroměstské náměstí and walk down to **Malé náměstí** (Small Square), a nearly perfect ensemble of facades dating from the Middle Ages. Note the Renaissance iron fountain dating from 1560 in the center of the square. The sgraffito on the house at No. 3 is not as old as it looks (1890), but here and there you can find authentic Gothic portals and Renaissance sgraffiti that betray the square's true age.

Look for tiny **Karlova ulice,** which begins in the southwest corner of Malé náměstí, and take another quick right to stay on it (watch the signs—this medieval street seems designed to confound the visitor). The character of Karlova ulice has changed in recent years to meet the growing number of tourists. Galleries and gift shops now occupy almost every storefront. But the cobblestones, narrow alleys, and crumbling gables still make it easy to imagine what life was like 400 years ago.

Turn left at the T-intersection in front of the Středočeská Galérie and continue left down the quieter Husova třída (if you want to go on directly to Tour 3, veer to the right for the Charles Bridge and the other side of the river). Fans of unbridled Baroque—the kind more common to Vienna than to Prague—may want to pause first and inspect the exotic **Clam–Gallas palota** (Clam-Gallas Palace) at Husova 20. You'll recognize it easily: Look for the Titans in the doorway holding up what must be a very heavy Baroque facade. The palace dates from 1713 and is the work of Johann Bernhard Fischer von Erlach, the famed Viennese virtuoso of the day. Enter the building (push past the guard as if you know what you're doing) for a glimpse of the finely carved stair-

case, the work of the master himself, and of the
Italian frescoes featuring Apollo that surround
it. The Gallas family was prominent during the
18th century but has long since died out. The
building now houses the municipal archives and
is rarely open to visitors.

Return to the T-intersection and continue down
Husova. For a glimpse of a less successful Baroque reconstruction, take a close look at the
16 **Kostel svatého Jiljí** (Church of St. Giles), across
from No. 7, another important outpost of Czech
Protestantism in the 16th century. The exterior
is powerful Gothic, including the buttresses and
a characteristic portal; the interior, surprisingly, is Baroque, dating from the 17th century.

Continue walking along Husova třída to Na
perštýně, and turn right at tiny Betlémská
ulice. The alley opens up onto a quiet square of
the same name (Betlémské náměstí) and upon
the most revered of all Hussite churches in
17 Prague, the **Betlémská kaple** (Bethlehem Chapel). The church's elegant simplicity is in stark
contrast to the diverting Gothic and Baroque of
the rest of the city. The original structure dates
from the end of the 14th century, and Hus himself was a regular preacher here from 1402 until
his death in 1415. After the Thirty Years' War
the church fell into the hands of the Jesuits and
was finally demolished in 1786. Excavations carried out after World War I uncovered the original portal and three windows, and the entire
church was reconstructed during the 1950s. Although little remains of the first church, some
remnants of Hus's teachings can still be read on
the inside walls. *Betlémské nám. 5. Admission
free. Open Apr.–Sept., daily 9–6; Oct.–Mar.,
daily 9–5.*

Return to Na Perštýně and continue walking to
the right. As you near the back of the buildings
of the busy **Národní třída** (National Boulevard),
turn left at Martinská ulice. At the end of the
18 street, the forlorn but majestic church **Kostel
svatého Martina ve zdi** (St. Martin-in-the-Wall)
stands like a postwar ruin. It's difficult to be-
lieve that this forgotten church, with a NO PARK-
ING sign blocking its main portal, once played a
major role in the development of Protestant prac-

tices. Still, it was here in 1414 that Holy Communion was first given to the Bohemian laity with both bread and the wine, in defiance of the Catholic custom of the time, which dictated that only bread was to be offered to the masses, with wine reserved for the priests and clergy. From then on, the chalice came to symbolize the Hussite movement.

Walk around the church to the left and through a little archway of apartments onto the bustling Národní třída. To the left, a five-minute walk away, lies Wenceslas Square and the starting point of the tour.

Time Out   Turn right instead of left onto Národní třída and head to the newly renovated **Café Slavia** (Národní třída 1, open daily 9–11), long considered one of Prague's most "literary" cafés. Enjoy the fine view of Prague Castle while sipping a coffee.

Tour 2: Josefov

Leave Staroměstské Náměsti (Old Town Square) via handsome Pařížská ulice and head north in the direction of the river and the Hotel Inter-Continental to reach **Josefov,** the Jewish quarter. The buildings and houses along Pařížská date from the end of the 19th century, and their elegant facades reflect the prosperity of the Czech middle classes at the time. Here and there you can spot the influence of the Viennese Jugendstil, with its emphasis on mosaics, geometric forms, and gold inlay. The look is fresh against the busier 19th-century revival facades of most of the other structures.

The festive atmosphere, however, changes suddenly as you enter the area of the ghetto. The buildings are lower here, and older; the mood is hushed. Sadly, little of the old ghetto remains. The Jews had survived centuries of discrimination, but two unrelated events of modern times have left the ghetto little more than a collection of museums. Around 1900, city officials decided for hygienic purposes to raze the ghetto and pave over its crooked streets. Only the synagogues, the town hall, and a few other buildings survived this early attempt at urban renewal. The second event was the Holocaust. Under Nazi occupation, a staggering percentage of Prague's Jews were deported or murdered in concentration camps. And of the 35,000 Jews living in the ghetto before World War II, only about 1,200 returned to resettle the neighborhood after the war.

The treasures and artifacts of the ghetto are now the property of the **Státní židovské muzeum** (State Jewish Museum), a complex comprising the Old Jewish Cemetery and the collections of the remaining individual synagogues. The holdings are vast, thanks, ironically, to Adolf Hitler, who had planned to open a museum here documenting the life and practices of what he had hoped would be an "extinct" people. The cemetery and most of the synagogues are open to the public. Each synagogue specializes in certain artifacts, and you can buy tickets for all the buildings at the **Vysoká synagóga** (High Synagogue), which features rich Torah mantles and silver. *Červená ulice (enter at No. 101). Tel. 02/ 231–0681. Admission: 20 Kč. adults, 10 Kč. students. Open Sun.–Fri. 10–12:30 and 1–6 (until 5 in winter).*

Adjacent to the High Synagogue, at Maislova 18, is the **Židovská radnice** (Jewish Town Hall), now home to the Jewish Community Center. The hall was the creation of Mordecai Maisel, an influential Jewish leader at the end of the 16th century. It was restored in the 18th century and given its clock and bell tower at that time. A second clock, with Hebrew numbers, turns to the left. The building also houses Prague's only kosher restaurant, Shalom.

The **Staronová synagóga** (Old-New Synagogue) across the street at Červená 2 is the oldest standing synagogue in Europe. Dating from the middle of the 13th century, it is also one of the most important works of early Gothic in Prague. The odd name recalls the legend that the synagogue was built on the site of an ancient Jewish temple and that stones from the temple were used to build the present structure. The synagogue has not only survived fires and the razing of the ghetto at the end of the last century but also emerged from the Nazi occupation intact and is still in active use. The oldest part of the synagogue is the entrance, with its vault supported by two pillars. The grille at the center of the hall dates from the 15th century. Note that men are required to cover their heads inside, and that during services men and women sit apart.

Continue along Červená ulice, which becomes the little street **U starého hřbitova** (At the Old Cemetery) beyond Maislova ulice. At the bend in the road lies the Jewish ghetto's most astonishing sight, the **Starý židovský hřbitov** (Old Jewish Cemetery). From the 14th century to 1787, all Jews living in Prague found their final resting place in this tiny, melancholy space not far from the busy city. Some 12,000 graves in all are piled atop one another in 12 layers. Walk the paths amid the gravestones. The relief symbols represent the name or profession of the deceased. The oldest marked grave belongs to the poet Avigdor Kara, who died in 1439. The best-known marker is probably that of Jehuda ben Bezalel, the famed Rabbi Loew, who is credited with having created the mythical Golem in 1573. Even today, small scraps of paper bearing wishes are stuffed into the cracks of the rabbi's tomb in the hope that he will grant them. Loew's grave lies just a few steps from the entrance, near the western wall of the cemetery.

Just to the right of the cemetery entrance is the **Obřadní síň** (Ceremony Hall), which houses a moving exhibition of drawings made by children held at the Nazi concentration camp at Terezín (Theresienstadt), in northern Bohemia. During the early years of the war the Nazis used the camp for propaganda purposes to demonstrate their "humanity" toward the Jews, and prisoners were given relative freedom to lead "normal" lives. Transports to death camps in Poland began in earnest in the final months of the war, however, and many thousands of Terezín prisoners, including many of these children, eventually perished . *U starého hřbitov. Admission to cemetery and Ceremony Hall: 20 Kč. adults, 10 Kč. children and students. Cemetery and hall open Sun.–Fri. 9–5 (until 4:30 in winter).*

Further testimony to the appalling crimes perpetrated against the Jews during World War II can be seen in the **Pinkasova synagóga** (Pinkas Synagogue), a handsome Gothic structure whose foundation dates from the 11th century. The names of 77,297 Bohemian and Moravian Jews murdered by the Nazis were inscribed in rows on the walls inside. Many of the names, sadly, were destroyed by water damage over the years. Enter the synagogue from Široká street on the other side of the cemetery. *Admission: 20 Kč. adults, 10 Kč. students. Open Sun.–Fri. 10–12:30 and 1–6 (until 5 in winter).*

Time Out U **Rudolfa** (Maislova 5) specializes in grilled meats, prepared before your eyes. Time your visit for off hours, however; the tiny restaurant fills up quickly. If there's no room, U **Golema** (Maislova 8) offers a strange mixture of Jewish, but not kosher, delicacies, including tasty Elixir Soup.

Return to Maislova ulice via U starého hřbitova, and turn right in the direction of the Old Town once again, crossing Široká ulice. Look in at the **②** **Maislova synagóga** (Maisel Synagogue), which houses an enormous collection of silver articles of worship confiscated by the Nazis from synagogues throughout Central Europe. Here you'll find the State Jewish Museum's finest collection of Torah wrappers and mantles, silver pointers, breastplates and spice boxes, candle holders (the eight-branched Hanukkiah and the seven-branched menorah), and Levite washing sets. *Maislova 10. Admission: 20 Kč. adults, 10 Kč. students. Open Sun.–Fri. 10–12:30 and 1–6 (until 5 in winter).*

Tour 3: Charles Bridge and Malá Strana

Prague's **Malá Strana** (the so-called Little Quarter) is not for the methodical tourist. Its charm lies in the tiny lanes, the sudden blasts of bombastic architecture, and the soul-stirring views that emerge for a second before disappearing behind the sloping roofs. The area is at its best in the evening, when the softer light hides the crumbling facades and brings you into a world of glimmering beauty.

❷❸ Begin the tour on the Old Town side of **Karlův
most** (the Charles Bridge), which you can reach
by foot in about 10 minutes from Staroměstské
náměstí. The view from the foot of the bridge is
nothing short of breathtaking, encompassing
the towers and domes of Malá Strana and the
soaring spires of the St. Vitus Cathedral to the
northwest. This heavenly vision, one of the most
beautiful in Europe, changes subtly in perspective as you walk across the bridge, attended by
the host of Baroque saints that decorates the
bridge's peaceful Gothic stones. At night its
drama is spellbinding: St. Vitus Cathedral lit in
a ghostly green, the castle in monumental yellow, and the Church of St. Nicholas in a voluptuous pink, all viewed through the menacing
silhouettes of the bowed statues and the Gothic
towers (if you do nothing else in Prague, you
must visit the Charles Bridge at night). During
the day the pedestrian bridge buzzes with activity. Street musicians vie with artisans hawking
jewelry, paintings, and glass for the hearts and
wallets of the passing multitude. At night the
crowds thin out a little, the musicians multiply,
and the bridge becomes a long block party—
nearly everyone brings a bottle.

When the Přemyslide princes set up residence
in Prague during the 10th century, there was a
ford across the Vltava at this point, a vital link
along one of Europe's major trading routes. After several wooden bridges and the first stone
bridge had washed away in floods, Charles IV
appointed a 27-year-old German, Peter Parler,
architect of St. Vitus Cathedral, to build a new
structure in 1357. After 1620, following the defeat of Czech Protestants by Catholic
Habsburgs at the Battle of White Mountain, the
bridge and its adornment became caught up in
the Catholic–Hussite (Protestant) conflict. The
many Baroque statues, built by Catholics and
which began to appear in the late 17th century,
eventually came to symbolize the totality of the
Austrian (hence Catholic) triumph. The Czech
writer Milan Kundera sees the statues from this
perspective: "The thousands of saints looking
out from all sides, threatening you, following
you, hypnotizing you, are the raging hordes of
occupiers who invaded Bohemia three hundred

and fifty years ago to tear the people's faith and language from their hearts."

The religious conflict is less obvious nowadays, leaving only the artistic tension between Baroque and Gothic that gives the bridge its allure. The **Old Town Bridge Tower** was where Paler began his bridge-building. The carved facades he designed for the sides of the bridge were destroyed by Swedish soldiers in 1648, at the end of the Thirty Years' War. The sculptures facing the square, however, are still intact; they depict the old gout-ridden Charles IV with his son, who later became Wenceslas IV. The climb of 138 steps is well worth the effort for the views it affords of the Old Town and, across the river, of Malá Strana and Prague Castle. *Admission: 20 Kč. adults, 10 Kč. children and students. Open Apr.–Oct., daily 9–6.*

It's worth pausing to take a closer look at some of the statues as you walk toward Malá Strana. The third on the right, a brass crucifix with Hebrew lettering in gold, was mounted on the location of a wooden cross that was destroyed in the battle with the Swedes (the golden lettering was reputedly financed by a Jew accused of defiling the cross). The eighth statue on the right, St. John of Nepomuk, is the oldest of all; it was designed by Johann Brokoff in 1683. On the left-hand side, sticking out from the bridge between the ninth and tenth statues (the latter has a wonderfully expressive vanquished Satan), stands a Roland statue. This knightly figure, bearing the coat of arms of the Old Town, was once a reminder that this part of the bridge belonged to the Old Town before Prague became a unified city in 1784. The square below is the Kampa Island, separated from the Lesser Town by an arm of the Vltava known as Čertovka (Devil's Stream) *(see below)*.

In the eyes of most art historians, the most valuable statue is the twelfth, on the left. Mathias Braun's statue of St. Luitgarde depicts the blind saint kissing Christ's wounds. The most compelling grouping, however, is the second from the end on the left, a work of Ferdinand Maximilien Brokov from 1714. Here the saints are incidental; the main attraction is the Turk, his face expressing extreme boredom while guarding Christians imprisoned in the cage at his side. When the statue was erected, just 29 years after the second Turkish invasion of Vienna, it scandalized the Prague public, who smeared the statue with mud.

By now you are almost at the end of the bridge. In front of you is the striking conjunction of the **24** two **Malá Strana Bridge Towers,** one Gothic, the other Romanesque. Together they frame the Baroque flamboyance of the St. Nicholas Church in the distance. At night this is an absolutely wondrous sight. The lower, Romanesque tower formed a part of the earlier wooden and stone bridges, its present appearance stemming from a renovation in 1591. The Gothic tower, **Mostecká věž,** was added to the bridge a few decades after its completion. If you didn't climb the tower on the Old Town side of the bridge, it's worth scrambling up the wooden stairs inside this tower for the views over the roofs of the Malá Strana and of the Old Town across the river. *Mostecká ul. Admission: 20 Kč. adults, 10 Kč. children and students. Open Apr.–Oct., daily 9–6.*

Walk under the gateway of the towers into the little uphill street called **Mostecká ulice.** You have now entered the **Malá Strana** (Little Quarter), established in 1257 and for years home to the merchants and craftsmen who served the royal court. Follow Mostecká ulice up to the rec-**25** tangular **Malostranské náměstí** (Little Quarter Square), now the district's traffic hub rather than its heart. The arcaded houses on the left, dating from the 16th and 17th centuries, exhibit a mix of Baroque and Renaissance elements. The beautiful blue building at No. 10, on the far side of the square, houses one of Prague's best restaurants, U Mecenáše (*see* Dining, *below*).

26 On the left side of the square stands **Chrám svatého Mikuláše** (St. Nicholas Church). With its dynamic curves, this church is one of the purest and most ambitious examples of High Baroque. The celebrated architect Christoph Dientzenhofer began the Jesuit church in 1704 on the site of one of the more active Hussite churches of 15th-century Prague. Work on the building was taken over by his son Kilian Ignaz Dientzenhofer, who built the dome and presbytery; Anselmo Lurago completed the whole in 1755 by adding the bell tower. The juxtaposition of the broad, full-bodied dome with the slender bell tower is one of the many striking architectural contrasts that mark the Prague skyline. Inside, the vast pink-and-green space is impossible to take in with a single glance; every corner bristles with movement, guiding the eye first to the dramatic statues, then to the hectic frescoes, and on to the shining faux-marble pillars. Many of the statues are the work of Ignaz Platzer; they constitute his last blaze of success. When the centralizing and secularizing reforms of Joseph II toward the end of the 18th century brought an end to the flamboyant Baroque era, Platzer's workshop was forced to declare bankruptcy. *Malostranské nám. Admission: 20 Kč. adults, 10 Kč. children and students. Open daily 9–4 (until 5 or 6 in summer).*

㉗ From Malostranské náměsti, turn left onto **Nerudova ulice,** named for the 19th-century Czech journalist and poet Jan Neruda (after whom Chilean poet Pablo Neruda renamed himself). This steep little street used to be the last leg of the Royal Way, walked by the king before his coronation, and it is still the best way to get to Prague Castle (*see* Tour 5, *below*). Until Joseph II's administrative reforms in the late 18th century, house numbering was unknown in Prague. Each house bore a name, depicted on the facade, and these are particularly prominent on Nerudova ulice. House No. 6, **U červeného orla** (At the Red Eagle), proudly displays a faded painting of a red eagle. Number 12 is known as **U tří housliček** (At the Three Violins). In the early 18th century, three generations of the Edlinger violin-making family lived here. Joseph II's scheme numbered each house according to its position in Prague's separate "towns" (here, Malá Strana) rather than according to its sequence on the street. The red plates record these original house numbers; the blue ones are the numbers used in addresses today.

Time Out Nerudova is filled with little restaurants and snack bars and offers something for everyone. U zeleného čaje at No. 19 is a fragrant little tea room, offering fruit and herbal teas as well as light salads and sweets. U Kocoura at No. 2 is a traditional pub that hasn't caved in to touristic niceties.

Two palaces break the unity of the burghers' houses on Nerudova. Both were designed by the adventurous Baroque architect Giovanni Santini, one of the Italian builders most in demand by wealthy nobles of the early 18th century. The **Morzin Palace,** on the left at No. 5, is now the Romanian embassy. The fascinating facade, with an allegory of night and day, was created in 1713 and is the work of F. M. Brokov of Charles Bridge statue fame. Across the street at No. 20 is the **Thun-Hohenstein Palace,** now the Italian Embassy. The gateway with two enormous eagles (the emblem of the Kolovrat family, who owned the building at the time) is the work of the other great Charles Bridge statue builder, Mathias Braun. Santini himself lived at No. 14, the so-called **Valkoun House.**

28 While you're at this end of the street, it's worth taking a quick look at the Rococo **Bretfeld palác** (Bretfeld Palace), No. 33, on the corner of Nerudova ulice and Janský vršek. The relief of St. Nicholas on the facade is the work of Ignaz Platzer, but the building is valued more for its historical associations than for its architecture: This is where Mozart, his lyricist partner Lorenzo da Ponte, and the aging but still infamous philanderer and music lover Casanova stayed at the time of the world premiere of *Don Giovanni* in 1787. The Malá Strana recently gained a new connection with Mozart when its streets were used to represent 18th-century Vienna in the filming of Miloš Forman's *Amadeus.*

Go back down a few houses until you come to the archway at No. 13, more or less opposite the Santini **Kostel Panny Marie ustavičné pomoci u Kajetánů** (Church of Our Lady of Perpetual Help at the Theatines). The archway, marked *Restaurace,* hides one of the many winding passageways that give Malá Strana its enchantingly ghostly character at night. Follow the dog-leg curve downhill, past two restaurants, vine-covered walls, and some broken-down houses. The alleyway really comes into its own only in the dark, the dim lighting hiding the grime and highlighting the mystery.

29 You emerge from the passageway at the top of **Tržiště ulice,** opposite the **Schönbornský palác** (Schönborn Palace). Franz Kafka had an apartment in this building from March through August 1917, after moving out from Zlatá ulička (Golden Lane) (*see* Tour 5). The U.S. Embassy now occupies this prime location. If you look through the gates, you can see the beautiful formal gardens rising up to the Petřin hill; they are unfortunately not open to the public.

Follow Tržiště downhill until you come to the main road, **Karmelitská ulice.** Here on your right is No. 25, an unobtrusive door hiding the **30** entranceway to the intimate **Vrtbovský palác** (Vrtba Palace and Gardens). Walk through the courtyard between the two Renaissance houses, the one to the left built in 1575, the one to the right in 1591. The owner of the latter house was one of the 27 Bohemian nobles executed by the Habsburgs in 1621 (*see* Tour 1). The house was given as confiscated property to Count Sezima of Vrtba, who bought the neighboring property and turned the buildings into a late-Renaissance palace. The *Vrtbovská zahrada* (Vrtba Gardens) boasts one of the best views over the Malá Strana rooftops and is a fascinating oasis from the tourist beat. Unfortunately, the gardens are perpetually closed for renovation, even though there is no sign of work in progress. The powerful stone figure of Atlas that caps the entranceway dates from 1720 and is the work of Mathias Braun. *Karmelitská ul. 25.*

Continue walking along Karmelitská until you reach the comfortably ramshackle **Kostel Panny Marie vítězné** (Church of Our Lady of Victories), the unlikely home of one of Prague's best-known religious artifacts, the Pražské Jezuliatko (Infant Jesus of Prague). Originally brought to Prague from Spain in the 16th century, this tiny porcelain doll (now bathed in neon lighting straight out of Las Vegas) is renowned world-

wide for showering miracles on devoted suppli-
cants. Nuns from a nearby convent arrive at
dawn each day to change the infant's clothes;
pieces of the doll's extensive wardrobe have
been sent by believers from around the world.
Karmelitská 9a. Admission free.

Cross over Karmelitská and walk down tiny
Prokopská ulice, opposite the Vrtba Palace. On
the left is the former Baroque **Church of St. Pro-
copius,** now oddly converted into an apartment
block. At the end of the lane you'll emerge onto
③ the peaceful **Maltézské náměstí** (Maltese
Square), named for the Knights of Malta. In the
middle of the square is a sculpture depicting
John the Baptist. This work, by Ferdinand
Brokov, was erected in 1715 to commemorate
the end of a plague. The relief on the far side
shows Salome engrossed in her dance of the
seven veils while John is being decapitated.
There are two intricately decorated palaces on
this square, to the right the Rococo Turba Palace, now the Japanese Embassy, and at the bottom, the Nostitz Palace, the Dutch Embassy.

③ Follow Lázeňská street to the **Velkopřevorské
náměstí** (Grand Priory Square). The palace
fronting the square is considered one of the finest Baroque buildings in the Malá Strana,
though it is now part of the Maltese Embassy
and no longer open to the public. Opposite the
palace is the flamboyant orange-and-white stuc-
co facade of the Buquoy Palace, built in 1719 by
Giovanni Santini and the present home of the
French Embassy. From the street you can
glimpse an enormous twinkling chandelier
through the window, but this is about all you'll
get to see of the elegant interior.

Across from this pompous display of Baroque
③ finery stands the **Lennon Peace Wall,** a peculiar
monument to the passive rebellion of Czech
youth against the strictures of the former communist regime. Under the Communists, Western rock music was officially discouraged, and
students adopted the former Beatle as a symbol
of resistance. Paintings of John Lennon and lyrics from his songs in Czech and English began to
appear on the wall sometime in the 1980s. Even
today, long after the Communists have de-

parted, new graffiti still turns up regularly. It's not clear how long the police or the owners of the wall will continue to tolerate the massive amounts of writing (which has started to spread to other walls around the neighborhood), but the volume of writing suggests that the Lennon myth continues to endure.

At the lower end of the square, a tiny bridge takes you across the **Čertovka** tributary to **❸④ Kampa Island.** The name Čertovka translates as Devil's Stream and reputedly refers to a cranky old lady who once lived on Maltese Square (given the river's present filthy state, however, the name is ironically appropriate). A right turn around the corner brings you to the foot of **Kampa Gardens,** whose unusually well-kept lawns are one of the few places in Prague where sitting on the grass is openly tolerated. If it's a warm day, spread out a blanket and bask for a while in the sunshine. The row of benches that line the river to the left is also a popular spot from which to contemplate the city. At night this stretch along the river is especially romantic.

Make your way north toward the Charles Bridge by following either Na Kampě or the network of small streets running parallel to the river. Walk underneath the Charles Bridge and onto the street named **U lužického semináře.** This area is known as the Venice of Prague. The house at No. 1 is the inn U tří Pštrosů (The Three Ostriches), one of Prague's oldest and most charming hotels. The original building stems from the 16th century, when one of the early owners was a supplier of ostrich feathers to the royal court. The top floors and curlicue gables were early Baroque additions from the 17th century. The inn was the site of the first coffeehouse in Prague, opened by the Armenian Deodat Damajian in 1714.

Time Out At the corner of Na Kampě, right next to the arches of the Charles Bridge, the small stand-up café **Bistro Bruncvík** (No. 7) serves hot wine and coffee in winter and cold drinks in summer. Its slices of pizza also are satisfying.

Continue along this Old World street, past a small square, until you reach a gate that marks **35** the entrance to **Vojanovy sady,** once the gardens of the Monastery of the Discalced Carmelites, later taken over by the Order of the English Virgins and now part of the Ministry of Finance (entrance on Letenská). With its weeping willows, fruit trees, and benches, the park is another peaceful haven in summer. Exhibitions of modern sculptures are often held here, contrasting sharply with the two Baroque chapels and the graceful Ignaz Platzer statue of John of Nepomuk standing on a fish at the entrance. The park is surrounded by the high walls of the old monastery and new Ministry of Finance buildings, with only an occasional glimpse of a tower or spire to remind you that you're in Prague. *Open daily 8–5 (until 7 in summer).*

Continue north along U lužického semináře, bearing left along the main road briefly until the intersection with **Letenská ulice,** which veers off to the left. If you've had enough sightseeing, you can easily return to the Old Town via the metro from here (Malostranská station).

Otherwise, even though it is open only during **36** summer, the **Zahrada Valdštejnského paláca** (Wallenstein Gardens) merit a short visit. Albrecht von Wallenstein, onetime owner of the house and gardens, began a meteoric military career in 1624 when the Austrian emperor Ferdinand II retained him to save the empire from the Swedes and Protestants during the Thirty Years' War. Wallenstein, wealthy by marriage, offered to raise 20,000 men at his own cost and lead them personally. Ferdinand II accepted and showered Wallenstein with confiscated land and titles. Wallenstein's first acquisition was this enormous area, where in 1623, having knocked down 23 houses, a brick factory, and three gardens, he began to build his magnificent palace (*Valdštejnský palác,* now government buildings closed to the public), with its idiosyncratic high-walled gardens. Walking around the formal paths, you'll come across numerous statues, an unusual fountain with a woman spouting water from her breasts, and a lava-stone grotto along the wall. *Off Letenská ul. Admission free. Open May 1–Sept. 30, daily 9–7.*

From here one option is to walk straight back down Letenská ulice to the Malostranská metro station. A more attractive route would take you up Letenská (past the U svatého Tomáše pub, where you can get wonderful dark beer), right on Tomášská ulice into Valdštejnské náměstí and down the exquisitely Baroque Valdštejnská ulice, ending up back at the Malostranské station, near the intersection with Pod Brouskou.

Tour 4: Hradčany

To the west of Prague Castle is the residential **Hradčany** (Castle District), the town that during the early 14th century emerged out of a collection of monasteries and churches. The concentration of history packed into one small area makes Prague Castle and the Castle District challenging objects for visitors not versed in the ups and downs of Bohemian kings, religious uprisings, wars, and oppression. The picturesque area surrounding Prague Castle, with its breathtaking vistas of Staré Město and Malá Strana, is ideal for just wandering; but the castle itself, with its convoluted history and architecture, is difficult to appreciate fully without investing a little more time, which is why we cover the castle on a separate tour (*see* Tour 5, *below*).

Our tour of the Castle District begins on Nerudova ulice, which runs east–west a few hundred yards south of Prague Castle. At the western foot of the street, look for a flight of stone steps guarded by two saintly statues. The stairs lead up to Loretánská ulice, affording panoramic views of St. Nicholas Church and Malá Strana. At the top of the steps, turn left and walk a couple hundred yards until you come **③** to a dusty elongated square named **Pohořelec** (Scene of Fire), the site of tragic fires in 1420, 1541, and 1741.

Time Out   Busy Pohořelec is a good place to grab a quick bite before tackling the castle. **Sate Grill** at No. 3 (open daily 11–8) offers a very passable Czech interpretation of Indonesian cooking in a stand-up, fast-food setting. At No. 11, **Caffe Calafuria** is an agreeable spot for coffee and a pastry.

Go through the inconspicuous gateway at No. 8
and up the steps, and you'll find yourself in the
(38) courtyard of the **Strahovský klášter** (Strahov
Monastery). Founded by the Premonstraten-
sian order in 1140, the monastery remained in
their hands until 1952, when the Communists
abolished all religious orders and turned the entire complex into the **Památník národního
písemnictví** (Museum of National Literature).
The major building of interest is the **Strahov Library,** with its collection of early Czech manu-
scripts, the 10th-century Strahov New
Testament, and the collected works of famed
Danish astronomer Tycho de Brahe. Also of note
is the late-18th-century **Philosophical Hall.** En-
gulfing its ceilings is a startling sky-blue fresco
completed by the Austrian painter Franz Anton
Maulbertsch in just six months. The fresco depicts an unusual cast of characters, including
Socrates' nagging wife Xanthippe, Greek astronomer Thales with his trusty telescope, and
a collection of Greek philosophers mingling with
Descartes, Diderot, and Voltaire. *Strahovské
nádvoří 132. Admission: 20 Kč. adults, 10 Kč.
children and students. Open daily 9–noon and
1–5.*

Retrace your steps to Loretánské náměstí,
which is flanked by the feminine curves of the
(39) Baroque **Loreto Church.** The church's seductive
lines were a conscious move on the part of
Counter-Reformation Jesuits in the 17th century who wanted to build up the cult of Mary and
attract the largely Protestant Bohemians back
to the church. According to legend, angels had
carried Mary's house in Nazareth and dropped
it in a patch of laurel trees in Ancona, Italy;
known as *Loreto* (from the Latin for laurel), it
immediately became a center of pilgrimage. The
Prague Loreto was one of many re-creations of
this scene across Europe, and it worked: Pil-
grims came in droves. The graceful facade, with
its voluptuous tower, was built in 1720 by Kilian
Ignaz Dientzenhofer, the architect of the two
St. Nicholas churches in Prague. Most spectac-
ular of all is a small exhibition upstairs displaying
the religious treasures presented to Mary in
thanks for various services, including a mon-
strance studded with 6,500 diamonds. *Loretán-*

*ské nám. 7, tel. 02/536-228. Admission: 30 Kč.
adults, 5 Kč. children and students. Open
Tues.–Sun. 9–12:15 and 1–4:30.*

Across the road, the 29 half-pillars of the
Černínský palác (Chernin Palace) now mask the
Czech Ministry of Foreign Affairs. During
World War II this ungainly palace was the seat
of the occupying German government. At the
bottom of Loretánské náměstí, a little lane trails
to the left into the area known as **Nový Svět**; the
name means "new world," though the district is
as Old World as they come. Turn right onto the
street Nový Svět. This picturesque winding little alley, with facades from the 17th and 18th
centuries, once housed Prague's poorest residents; now many of the homes are used as artists' studios. The last house on the street, No. 1,
was the home of the Danish-born astronomer
Tycho de Brahe. Living so close to the Loreto,
so the story goes, Tycho was constantly dis-
turbed during his nightly stargazing by the
church bells. He ended up complaining to his patron, Emperor Rudolf II, who instructed the
Capuchin monks to finish their services before
the first star appeared in the sky.

Continue around the corner, where you get a
tantalizing view of the cathedral through the
trees. Walk past the Austrian Embassy to
Kanovnická ulice, a winding street lined with
the dignified but melancholy **Kostel svatého
Jana Nepomuckého** (Church of St. John
Nepomuk). At the top of the street, on the left,
the rounded, Renaissance, corner house
Martinický palác (Martinic Palace) catches the
eye with its detailed sgraffito drawings.

40 Martinic Palace opens onto **Hradčanské náměstí**
(Hradčany Square). With its fabulous mixture
of Baroque and Renaissance housing, topped by
the castle itself, the square featured prominent-
ly (ironically, disguised as Vienna) in the film
Amadeus, directed by the exiled Czech director
Miloš Forman. The house at No. 7 was the set for
Mozart's residence, where the composer was
haunted by the masked figure he thought was
his father. Forman used the flamboyant Rococo
Arcibiskupský palác (Archbishop's Palace), at
the top of the square on the left, as the Viennese

archbishop's palace. The plush interior, shown off in the film, is open to the public only on Maundy Thursday.

To the left of the Archbishop's Palace is an alleyway leading down to the **Národní galérie** (National Gallery), housed in the 18th-century Šternberský palác (Sternberg Palace). You'll need at least an hour to view the palace's impressive art collection—one collection in Prague you should not miss. On the first floor there's an exhibition of icons and other religious art from the 3rd through the 14th centuries. Up a second flight of steps is an entire room full of Cranachs and an assortment of paintings from Holbein, Dürer, Brueghel, Van Dyck, Canaletto, and Rubens, not to mention works by modern masters like Picasso, Matisse, Chagall, and Kokoschka. *Hradčanské nám. 15, tel. 02/ 352441 or 02/534457. Admission: 40 Kč. adults, 10 Kč. children and students. Open Tues.–Sun. 10–6.*

Across the square, the handsome sgraffito sweep of **Schwarzenberg palota** (Schwarzenberg Palace) beckons; this is the building you saw from the back side at the beginning of the tour. The palace was built for the Lobkowitz family between 1545 and 1563; today it houses the **Vojenské muzeum** (Military Museum), one of the largest of its kind in Europe. Of more general interest are the jousting tournaments held in the courtyard in summer. *Hradčanské nám. 2. Admission: 20 Kč. adults, 10 Kč. children and students. Open May 1–Sept. 30, Tues.–Sun. 9–4:30.*

Tour 5: Prague Castle

Numbers in the margin correspond to points of interest on the Tour 5: Prague Castle (Pražský hrad) map.

Despite its monolithic presence, **Pražský Hrad** (Prague Castle) is a collection of buildings dating from the 10th to the 20th century, all linked by internal courtyards. The most important structures are St. Vitus Cathedral, clearly visible soaring above the castle walls, and the Royal Palace, the official residence of kings and presi-

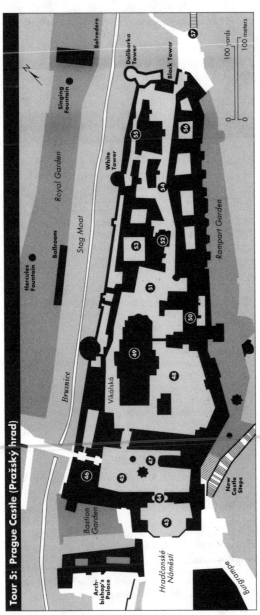

Tour 5: Prague Castle (Pražský hrad)

Bazilika Sv. Jiří (St. George's Basilica), **52**

Chrám Sv. Víta (St. Vitus Cathedral), **49**

Druhé Nádvoří (Second Courtyard), **45**

Hradní Galérie (Castle Gallery), **46**

Jiřská Ulice (St. George's Lane), **54**

Jiřské Náměstí (St. George's Square), **51**

Kaple Sv. Kříže (Chapel of the Holy

Klášter Sv. Jiří (St. George's Convent), **53**

Královský Palác (Royal Palace), **50**

Lobkovický Palác, **56**

Matyášova Brána (Matthias Gate), **44**

První Nádvoří (First Courtyard), **43**

Staré Zámecké Schody (Old Castle Steps), **57**

Třetí Nádvoří (Third Courtyard), **48**

Zlatá Ulička (Golden

dents and still the center of political power in the Czech Republic.

The main entrance to Prague Castle from Hradčanské náměstí is a little disappointing. Going through the wrought-iron gate, guarded at ground level by pristine Czech soldiers and from above by the ferocious *Battling Titans* (a copy of Ignaz Platzer's original 18th-century statues), you'll enter the **První nádvoří** (First Courtyard), built on the site of old moats and gates that once separated the castle from the surrounding buildings and thus protect the vulnerable western flank. This courtyard is one of the more recent additions to the castle, commissioned by the Habsburg empress Maria Theresa and designed by her court architect Nicolò Pacassi during the 1760s. Today it forms part of the presidential office complex. Pacassi's reconstruction was intended to unify the eclectic collection of buildings that made up the castle. From a distance, the effect is monumental. As you move farther into the castle, large parts appear to be relatively new, while in reality they cover splendid Gothic and Romanesque interiors.

44 It is worth looking closely at **Matyášova brána** (Matthias Gate) before going through to the next courtyard. Built in 1614, the stone gate once stood alone in front of the moats and bridges that surrounded the castle. Under the Habsburgs, the gate survived by being grafted as a relief onto the palace building. As you go through the gate, notice the ceremonial white-marble entrance halls on either side. These lead up to President Václav Havel's reception rooms, which are not open to the public.

45 The **Druhé nádvoří** (Second Courtyard) was the major victim of Pacassi's attempts at imparting classical grandeur to the castle. Except for the view of the spires of St. Vitus Cathedral towering above the palace, there's little for the eye to feast upon here. Built during the late-16th and early 17th centuries, this courtyard was part of an even earlier reconstruction program commissioned by Rudolf II, under whom Prague enjoyed a period of unparalleled cultural development. Once the Prague court was established, the emperor gathered around him some of the worlds's best craftsmen, artists, and scientists, including the brilliant astronomers Johannes Kepler and Tycho de Brahe.

Rudolf also amassed a large collection of art, surveying instruments, and coins. The bulk of the collection was looted by the Swedes and Habsburgs during the Thirty Years' War or auctioned off during the 18th century, but a small part of the collection was rediscovered in unused castle rooms during the 1960s and is now on display in the **Hradní galérie** (Castle Gallery), on the left side of the Second Courtyard. Apart from works by such world-famous artists as Titian, Rubens, and Tintoretto, look for the rarer works of Rudolf's court painters Hans von Aachen and Bartolomeo Spranger, and of the Bohemian Baroque painters Jan Kupecký and Petr Brandl. The passageway at the gallery entrance is the northern entrance to the castle and leads out over a luxurious ravine known as the **Jeleni příkop** (Stag Moat). *Admission: 10 Kč. adults, 5 Kč. children and students. Open Tues.–Sun. 10–6 (until 5:30 in winter).*

The Second Courtyard also houses the religious reliquary of Charles IV inside the **Kaple svatého Kříže** (Chapel of the Holy Cross). Displays include Gothic silver busts of the major Bohemian patron saints and a collection of bones and vestments that supposedly belonged to various saints. *Admission: 10 Kč. adults, 5 Kč. children and students. Open Tues.–Sun. 9–4 (until 5 in summer).*

Through the passageway on the far wall you'll come to the **Třetí nádvoří** (Third Courtyard). As you enter, the graceful soaring towers of **Chrám svatého Víta** (St. Vitus Cathedral) command your attention and admiration. The Gothic cathedral, among the most beautiful in Europe, has a long and complicated history, beginning during the 10th century and continuing to its completion in 1929. If you want to hear more about the ins and outs, English-speaking guided tours of the cathedral and the Royal Palace (*see below*) can be arranged at the Information Office around the left side of the cathedral, past the Vikářka restaurant.

Once you enter the cathedral, pause to take in
the vast but delicate beauty of the Gothic interi-
or, glowing in the colorful light that filters
through the startlingly brilliant stained-glass
windows. This back half, including the western
facade and the two towers you can see from outside, was not completed until 1929, following
the initiative of the Union for the Completion of
the Cathedral set up in the last days of the 19th
century. Don't let the neo-Gothic delusion keep
you from examining this new section. The six
stained-glass windows to your left and right and
the large rose window behind are modern mas-
terpieces. Take a good look at the third window
up on the left. The familiar Art Nouveau flamboyance, depicting the blessing of the 9th-
century St. Cyril and St. Methodius (missionaries to the Slavs and creators of the Cyrillic alphabet), is the work of the Czech father of the
style, Alfons Mucha. He achieved the subtle col-
oring by painting rather than staining the glass.

If you walk a little farther, just past the entrance to your right, you will find the exquisitely ornate **Chapel of St. Wenceslas.** This square
chapel, with a 14th-century tomb holding the
saint's remains, is the ancient heart of the cathedral. Wenceslas (the "good king" of Christmas-
carol fame) was a determined Christian in an era
of widespread paganism. In 925, as prince of Bohemia, he founded a rotunda church dedicated
to St. Vitus on this site. But the prince's brother, Boleslav, was impatient to take power and
ambushed Wenceslas four years later near a
church north of Prague. Wenceslas was originally buried in that church, but his grave pro-
duced so many miracles that he rapidly became a
symbol of piety for the common people, something that greatly irritated the new Prince
Boleslav. In 931 Boleslav was finally forced to
honor his brother by reburying the body in the
St. Vitus Rotunda. Shortly after that, Wenceslas was canonized.

The cathedral's rotunda was replaced by a Romanesque basilica during the late 11th century.
Work was begun on the existing building in 1344
on the initiative of the man who was later to become Charles IV. For the first few years the
chief architect was the Frenchman Mathias

d'Arras, but after his death, in 1352, the work was continued by the 22-year-old German architect Peter Parler, who went on to build the Charles Bridge and many other Prague treasures.

The small door in the back of the chapel leads to the **Crown Chamber,** the repository of the Bohemian crown jewels. It remains locked with seven keys held by seven different people and is definitely not open to the public.

A little beyond the Wenceslas Chapel on the same side, a small cash desk marks the entrance to the **underground crypt** (admission: 5 Kč.), interesting primarily for the information it provides about the cathedral's history. As you descend the stairs, on the right you'll see parts of the old Romanesque basilica. A little farther, in a niche to the left, are parts of the foundations of the rotunda. Moving around into the second room, you'll find a rather eclectic group of royal remains ensconced in new sarcophagi dating from the 1930s. In the center is Charles IV, who died in 1378. Rudolf II, patron of Renaissance Prague, is entombed at the rear. To his right is Maria Amalia, the only child of Maria Theresa to reside in Prague. Ascending the wooden steps back into the cathedral, you'll come to the white marble **Royal Mausoleum,** atop which lie stone statues of the first two Habsburg kings to rule in Bohemia, Ferdinand I and Maximilian II.

The cathedral's **Royal Oratory** was used by the kings and their families when attending mass. Built in 1493, the work is a perfect example of the late-Gothic, laced on the outside with a stone network of gnarled branches very similar in pattern to the ceiling vaulting in the Royal Palace (*see below*). The oratory is connected to the palace by an elevated covered walkway, which you can see from outside.

From here you can't fail to catch sight of the ornate silver **sarcophagus of St. John of Nepomuk,** designed by the famous Viennese architect Fischer von Erlach. According to legend, when Nepomuk's body was exhumed in 1721 to be reinterred, the tongue was found to be still intact and pumping with blood. These strange tales sadly served a highly political purpose. The

Catholic church and the Habsburgs were seeking a new folk hero to replace the protestant Jan Hus, whom they despised. The late Father Nepomuk was sainted and reburied a few years later with great ceremony in the 3,700-pound silver tomb, replete with angels and cherubim; the tongue was enshrined in its own reliquary.

The chapels around the back of the cathedral, the work of the original architect, Mathias d'Arras, are unfortunately closed to the public. Opposite the wooden relief, depicting the looting of the cathedral by Protestants in 1619, is the **Wallenstein Chapel.** Since the last century, it has housed the Gothic tombstones of its two architects, Mathias d'Arras and Peter Parler, who died in 1352 and 1399, respectively. If you look up to the balcony you can just make out the busts of these two men, designed by Parler's workshop. The other busts around the triforium depict various Czech kings.

The Hussite wars in the 15th century put an end to the first phase of the cathedral's construction. During the short era of illusory peace before the Thirty Years' War, lack of money laid to rest any idea of finishing the building, and the cathedral was closed by a wall built across from the Wenceslas Chapel. Not until the 20th century was the western side of the cathedral, with its two towers, completed according to Parler's original plans. *St. Vitus Cathedral. Admission free. Open May–Sept., Tues.–Sun. 9–5; Oct.–Apr., Tues.–Sun. 9–4.*

The contrast between the cool, dark interior of the cathedral and the brightly colored Pacassi facades of the Third Courtyard is startling. The clean lines of the courtyard are Plečnik's work from the 1930s, but the modern look is a deception. Plečnik's paving was intended to cover an underground world of wooden houses, streets, and walls dating from the 9th through 12th century that was rediscovered when the cathedral was completed. Since these are not open to the public, we are left with the modern structure (supplemented recently by an exchange office). Plečnik did add a few eclectic features to catch the eye: a granite obelisk to commemorate the fallen of the First World War, a black marble pedestal for the Gothic statue of St. George (the original is in the museum), and the peculiar golden ball topping the eagle fountain that un-

50 obtrusively marks the entrance to the **Královský palác** (Royal Palace). There are two main points of interest inside the externally nondescript palace. The first is the **Vladislavský sál** (Vladislav Hall), the largest secular Gothic interior space in Central Europe. The enormous hall was completed in 1493 by Benedict Ried, who was to late–Bohemian Gothic what Peter Parler was to the earlier version. The room imparts a sense of space and light, softened by the sensuous lines of the vaulted ceilings and brought to a dignified close by the simple oblong form of the early Renaissance windows, a style that was just beginning to make inroads in Central Europe. In its heyday, the hall was the site of jousting tournaments, festive markets, banquets, and coronations. In more recent times, it has been used to inaugurate presidents, from the Communist Klement Gottwald in 1948 to Václav Havel in 1990.

From the front of the hall, turn right into the rooms of the **Česká kancelář** (Bohemian Chancellery). This wing was built by the same Benedict Ried only 10 years after the hall was completed, but it shows a much stronger Renaissance influence. Pass through the Renaissance portal into the last chamber of the Chancellery. This room was the site of the Second Prague Defenestration in 1618, an event that marked the beginning of the Bohemian rebellion and, ultimately, of the Thirty Years' War. This peculiarly Bohemian method of expressing protest (throwing someone out of a window) had first been used in 1419 in the New Town Hall, an event that led to the Hussite wars. Two hundred years later the same conflict was reexpressed in terms of Habsburg-backed Catholics versus Bohemian Protestants. Rudolf II had reached an uneasy agreement with the Bohemian nobles, allowing them religious freedom in exchange for financial support. But his successor, Ferdinand II, was a rabid opponent of Protestantism and disregarded Rudolf's tolerant "Letter of Majesty." Enraged, the Protestant nobles stormed the castle and Chancellery and threw two Catholic officials and their secretary, for good measure, out of the window. Legend has it that they landed on a mound of horse dung and escaped unharmed, an event that the Jesuits interpreted as a miracle. The square window in question is on the left as you enter the room.

The exit to the **Palace Courtyard** is halfway down the Vladislav Hall on the left. Before leaving, you might want to peek into some of the other rooms. At the back of the hall, a staircase leads up to a gallery of the **All Saints' Chapel.** Little remains of Peter Parler's original work, but the church contains some fine works of art. The large room to the left of the staircase is the **Stará sněmovna** (Council Chamber), where the Bohemian nobles met with the king in a kind of prototype parliament. Portraits of the Habsburg rulers line the walls. As you leave the palace, be sure to notice the gradually descending steps. This is the **Riders' Staircase** to the left of the Council Chamber; this was the entranceway for knights who came for the jousting tournaments. *Royal Palace, tel. 02/2101. Admission: 10 Kč. adults, 5 Kč. children and students. Open Tues.–Sun. 9–5 (until 4 in winter).*

The exit from the Royal Palace will bring you **51** out onto **Jiřské náměstí** (St. George's Square); at **52** its east end stands the Romanesque **Bazilika svatého Jiří** (St. George's Basilica). This church was originally built during the 10th century by Prince Vratislav I, the father of Prince (and St.) Wenceslas. It was dedicated to St. George (of dragon fame), who, it was believed, would be more agreeable to the still largely pagan people. The outside was remodeled during early Baroque times, although the striking rusty-red color is in keeping with the look of the original, 10th-century structure. The interior, however, following substantial renovation, looks more or less as it did in the 12th century and is the best-preserved Romanesque relic in the country. The effect is at once barnlike and peaceful, the warm golden yellow of the stone walls and the small triplet arched windows exuding a sense of enduring harmony. The house-shaped, painted tomb at the front of the church holds the remains of the founder, Vratislav I. Up the steps, in a chapel to the right, is the tomb Parler designed for St. Ludmila, the grandmother of St. Wenceslas. *Tel. 02/2101. Admission: 10 Kč. adults, 5 Kč. children and students. Open Tues.–Sun. 9–5 (until 4 in winter).*

Next to the basilica on the square is the former **❺❸ Klášter svatého Jiří** (St. George's Convent), which now houses the Old Bohemian Art Collection of the **Czech National Gallery.** The museum runs through the history of Czech art from the early Middle Ages, with exhibits that include religious statues, icons, and triptychs, as well as the rather more secular themes of the Mannerist school and the voluptuous work of the court painters of Rudolf II. *Tel. 02/535240 or 02/535246. Admission: 40 Kč. adults, 10 Kč. children and students. Open Tues.–Sun. 9–5:30.*

❺❹ Walk down **Jiřská ulice** (St. George's Lane) until you come to a street leading to the left. At the **❺❺** top is **Zlatá ulička** (Golden Lane), an enchanting collection of tiny, ancient, brightly colored houses with long, sloping roofs, crouching under the fortification wall and looking remarkably like a Disney set for *Snow White and the Seven Dwarfs.* Legend has it that these were the lodgings of the international group of alchemists whom Rudolf II brought to the court to produce gold. The truth is a little less romantic: The houses were built during the 16th century for the castle guards, who supplemented their income by practicing various crafts outside the jurisdiction of the powerful guilds. By the early 20th century, Golden Lane had become the home of poor artists and writers. Franz Kafka, who lived at No. 22 in 1916 and 1917, described the house on first sight as "so small, so dirty, impossible to live in and lacking everything necessary." But he soon came to love the place. As he wrote to his fiancée: "Life here is something special . . . to close out the world not just by shutting the door to a room or apartment but to the whole house, to step out into the snow of the silent lane." The lane now houses tiny stores selling books, music, and crafts.

Return to Jiřská ulice and continue on down to **❺❻ Lobkovický palác** (Lobkovitz Palace). From the beginning of the 17th century until the 1940s, this building was the residence of the powerful Catholic Lobkovitz family. It was to this house that the two defenestrated officials escaped after landing on the dung hill in 1618. During the 1970s the building was restored to its early Baroque appearance and now houses the permanent exhibition "Monuments of the Czech National Past." If you want to get a chronological understanding of Czech history from the beginnings of the Great Moravian Empire in the 9th century to the Czech national uprising in 1848, this is your chance. Copies of the crown jewels are on display here; but it is the rich collection of illuminated Bibles, old musical instruments, coins, weapons, royal decrees, paintings, and statues that makes the museum well worth visiting. Detailed information on the exhibits is available in English. *Admission: 10 Kč. adults, 5 Kč. children and students. Open Tues.–Sun. 9–5 (until 4 in winter).*

Turn right out of the Lobkovitz Palace and leave the castle grounds through the east gate. Take a look over the bastion on your right for one last great view of the city. From here, descend the **❺⑦** romantic, vine-draped **Staré zámecké schody** (Old Castle Steps), which come out just above the Malostranská metro station. A direct subway line runs from here to Wenceslas Square (Můstek station).

What to See and Do with Children

Prague's small but delightful **Zoologická zahrada** (zoo) is located north of the city in Troja, under the shadow of the Troja Castle. Take the metro line C to Nádraží Holešovice and change to Bus 112. *Admission: 30 Kč. adults, 10 Kč. children. Open May, daily 7–6; June–Sept., daily 7–7; Oct.–Apr., daily 7–3.*

An hour or two of **rowing on the Vltava** is a great way to spend a sunny afternoon in Prague. Boats are available for rent in season (May–September) on the island across from the embankment near the Národní Divadlo (National Theater) for 40 Kč. an hour.

One of the unique delights of Prague for children and adults alike is **feeding the swans** along the banks of the Vltava River, and one spot in

Malá Strana is especially popular. Walk to the right from the exit of the Malostranská metro stop and walk up the street called U lužického semináře. The riverbank is accessible to your left just before you get to the Vojanovy park on the right. The atmosphere here is festive, especially on weekends, and the views over the city are breathtaking.

There are no fewer than three **puppet theaters** in Prague, all of which perform primarily for young children. Ask at Čedok or your hotel for details of performances.

Off the Beaten Track

Kafka's Grave. Kafka's modest tombstone in the New Jewish Cemetery (Židovské hřbitovy), situated beyond Vinohrady in a rather depressing part of Prague, seems grossly inadequate to Kafka's stature but oddly in proportion to his own modest ambitions. The cemetery is usually open for visitors; guards sometimes inexplicably seal off the grounds, but you can still glimpse the grave through the gate's iron bars. Take the metro to Želivského, turn right at the main cemetery gate, and follow the wall for about 100 yards. Dr. Franz Kafka's thin, white tombstone lies at the front of section 21.

Kostel Najsvětějšího Srdca Pana (Church of the Most Sacred Heart). If you've had your fill of Romanesque, Gothic, and Baroque, take the metro to Vinohrady (Jiřího z Poděbrad station) for a look at this amazing Art Deco cathedral. Designed in 1927 by Slovenian architect Jože Plečnik, the same architect commissioned to update the Prague Castle, the church more resembles a luxury ocean liner than a place of worship. The effect was conscious; during the 1920s and '30s, the avant garde carefully imitated mammoth objects of modern technology. Plečnik used many modern elements on the inside: Notice the hanging speakers, seemingly designed to bring the word of God directly to the ears of each worshiper. You may be able to find someone at the back entrance of the church who will let you walk up the long ramp into the fascinating glass clock tower.

Letenské sady (Letna Gardens). Come to this large, shady park for an unforgettable view from on high of Prague's bridges. From the enormous cement pedestal at the center of the park, the largest statue of Stalin in Eastern Europe once beckoned to citizens on the Old Town Square far below. The statue was ripped down during the 1960s, when Stalinism was finally discredited. Now the ideology-weary city fathers don't quite know what to do with the space. The room below the base is occasionally used as a venue for rock music. The walks and grass that stretch out behind the pedestal are perfect for relaxing on a warm afternoon. On sunny Sundays expatriates often meet up here to play ultimate Frisbee. To get to Letna, cross the Svatopluka Čecha Bridge, opposite the Hotel Inter-Continental, and climb the stairs.

Petřín. For a superb view of the city—from a mostly undiscovered, tourist-free perch—take the small funicular up through the hills of the Malá Strana to Prague's own miniature version of the Eiffel Tower. To reach the funicular, cross the Leglí Bridge near the Národní Divadlo (National Theater), and walk straight ahead to the Petřín Park. You can use normal public transport tickets for the funicular. Although the tower is closed to visitors, the area with the broken-down hall of mirrors and seemingly abandoned church is beautifully peaceful and well worth an afternoon's wandering. For the descent, meander on foot down through the stations of the cross on the pathways leading back to the Malá Strana. If you branch off to the left in the direction of the Strahov Monastery, you'll get one of the best views of Prague, with the castle out to the left, embracing the roofs of the Malá Strana and the Old Town far below.

Villa Bertramka. Mozart fans won't want to pass up a visit to this villa, where the great composer lived when in Prague. The small, well-organized museum is packed with memorabilia, including the program from that exciting night in 1787 when *Don Giovanni* had its world premiere in Prague. Also on hand is one of the master's pianos. Take the metro line B to the Anděl station, walk down Plzeňská ulice a few hundred yards, and take a left at Mozartova ulice. *Mozartova ul. 169, Smíchov, tel. 02/543893. Admission: 20 Kč. adults, 10 Kč. children. Open daily 10–5.*

3 Shopping

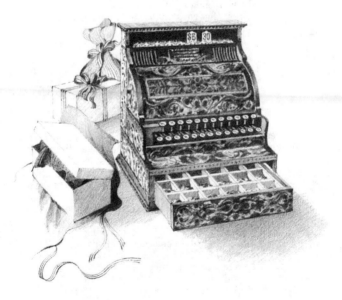

Despite the relative shortage of quality clothes—Prague has a long way to go before it can match the shopping meccas of Paris and Rome—the capital is a great place to pick up gifts and souvenirs. Bohemian crystal and porcelain deservedly enjoy a worldwide reputation for quality, and plenty of shops offer excellent bargains. The local market for antiques and artworks is still relatively undeveloped. In addition, the dozens of antiquarian bookshops can yield some excellent finds, particularly in German and Czech books and graphics. Another bargain is recorded music: LP and even CD prices are about half of what you would pay in the West.

Shopping Districts The major shopping areas are **Národní třída,** running past Můstek to Na příkopě, and the area around **Staroměstské náměstí** (Old Town Square). **Pařížská ulice, Karlova ulice** (on the way to the Charles Bridge), and the area just south of **Josefov** (the Jewish Quarter) are also good places to try boutiques and antiques shops. In the Malá Strana, try **Nerudova ulice,** the street that runs up to the Castle Hill district.

Department Stores These are generally well stocked, and, if you're willing to push through the crowds, will yield some interesting finds and bargains. The best are **Kotva** (Nám. republiky 8, tel. 02/2480–1111), **Kmart** (Národní třída 26, tel. 02/2422–7971), **Bílá Labuť** (Na poříčí 23, tel. 02/2481–1364), and **Krone** (Václavské nám. 21, tel. 02/2426–0477).

Street Markets For fruits and vegetables, the best street market in central Prague is on **Havelská ulice** in the Old Town. Stalls stock crafts, spices, and groceries but mostly the same fruits and vegetables in every season at the same prices. The best market for nonfood items is the vast, outdoor **Pražská tržnice** (Prague Marketplace) in the neighborhood of Holešovice, north of the city center, where you'll find everything from stereo equipment to ski gear and leather jackets. Take metro line C to the Vltavská station, and then ride any tram heading east (running to the left as you exit the metro station). Exit at the first stop, and follow the crowds.

Specialty *Starožitnosti* (antiques shops) are everywhere
Stores in Prague, but you'll need a sharp eye to distin-
Antiques guish truly valuable pieces from merely interesting ones. Many dealers carry old glassware
and vases. Antique jewelry, many pieces featuring garnets, is also popular. Remember to retain
your receipts as proof of legitimate purchases,
otherwise you may have difficulty bringing antiques out of the country. Comparison shop at
stores along Karlova ulice in the Old Town. Also
check in and around the streets of the Jewish
Ghetto for shops specializing in Jewish antiques
and artifacts. **Art Program** (Nerudova ul. 28) in
the Malá Strana has an especially beautiful collection of Art Deco jewelry and glassware.

Books and It's hard to imagine a more beautiful bookstore
Prints than **U Karlova Mostu** (Karlova ul. 2, Staré
Město, tel. 02/2422–9205), with its impressive
selection of old maps and prints, rare books, and
even current copies of the *New York Review of
Books*. One shop that comes close is **Antikvariát
Karel Křenek** (Celetná 31, tel. 02/232–2919),
near the Powder Tower in the Old Town. It
stocks prints and graphics from the 1920s and
'30s, in addition to a small collection of English
books. The **Melantrich** (Na příkopě 3, tel. 02/
267166) is a small but excellent source for high-
quality art and graphics books. The store also
stocks a full set of maps to most Czech cities,
auto atlases, and English-language magazines
and newspapers.

The **Globe Bookstore** (Janovského 14, Prague 7,
tel. 02/255–7462), north of the Old Town in
Holešovice, has helped put Prague on the map
as the "Left Bank of the '90s." You'll feel as if
you just stepped into the living room of a slightly addled, brilliant professor. Visitors could
spend an entire day and evening at the Globe,
drifting from the shelves to the adjacent café
and back again. If you can't find the book you're
looking for here, chances are you won't find it in
Prague. Check the bulletin board at the back of
the shop to find out what Prague's American-
English community is up to. The café has
yummy, healthy food at reasonable prices. A
close contender for best bookstore in Prague is
U Knihomola (Manesova 79, Prague 2, tel. 02/
627–7770). The "Bookworm" prides itself on

carrying English-language books on every possible subject. Downstairs is a bistro that serves everything from espresso to a French cheese plate to extravagant champagnes.

Big Ben Bookshop (Rybná 2, Staré Město, tel. 02/232–8249) has lots of paperback novels and an excellent selection of Agatha Christie mysteries. A small shop tucked inside the main building of Charles University, **Bohemian Ventures** (Nám. Jana Palacha, Staré Město, tel. 02/231–9516) stocks many English and American classics. **Frapas Literary Café Club** (Husova 9, Staré Město, tel. 02/2421–0870) is as much a state of mind as a bookstore. Classical music wafts through the shelves as you browse the respectable selection, which includes a good number of English-language novels. The quiet café next door sponsors regular readings and informal jazz concerts.

Crystal and Porcelain **Moser** (Na příkopě 12, tel. 02/2421–1293), the flagship store for the world-famous Karlovy Vary glassmaker, is the first address for stylish, high-quality lead crystal and china. Even if you're not in the market to buy, stop by the store simply to browse through the elegant wood-paneled salesrooms on the second floor. The staff will gladly pack goods for traveling. **Bohemia** (Pařížska 2, tel. 02/2481–1023) carries a wide selection of porcelain from Karlovy Vary. **Cristallino** (Celetná 12, Staré Město, tel. 02/261–216) will safely ship your purchases anywhere in the world. Their hand-cut wine glasses and vases make handsome wedding presents. **Furalo** (Václavské nám. 60, tel. 02/2422–0177) carries every sort of crystal, from the gaudy to the gilded, from classic-cut to minimalist styles, and will also oblige customers with careful packing and shipping. If you still can not find anything, have no fear: There is a crystal shop on just about every street in central Prague.

Food Specialty food stores were slow to catch on in Prague, but now they're everywhere. **Fruits de France** (Jindřišská 9, Nové Město, tel. 02/421–6882) is one of the best. Fresh lichees, asparagus, bean sprouts, avocados, and every other kind of "exotic" vegetable and fruit are stocked in ample quantities. Brie, Münster, and Saint-

Nectaire compete for attention at the cheese counter. Most of the products here, including yogurts and preserves, are imported directly from France, and, unfortunately, for sale at Western prices.

If you're looking for something extra special for a picnic lunch, Prague also has some excellent gourmet shops. **Dona-D** (Liliova 15, Staré Město) is a Spanish café and food shop that offers a small selection of Spanish wines, coffee, and chocolate, as well as tangy olives and savory stuffed anchovies. All of the wines can be sampled by the glass at the café. You may well feel as if you're in France at the **Paris Praha French Deli and Café** (Jindřišská 7, Nové Město, tel. 02/ 2422–2855), which tempts with pastries, French mustards and dressings, seafood, prepared salads, and cheese, plus French wines and pâtés. **Košer Potraviny** (Kosher Grocery Store, Břehova 5/274, Staré Město) carries a small selection of dried foods and kosher bread.

Prague has yet to launch a gourmet coffee emporium, but tea lovers are well cared for at **Dobrá čajovna** (Václavské nám. 14, Nové Město, tel. 02/ 2423–1480), which has a superb selection of Japanese, Chinese, South American, and African teas; the various brews can be sampled in the café. **Hisho** Japanese food shop (Havelská 6, Staré Město, tel. 02/2423–2056) purveys delightful Japanese delicacies, from kelp to eels, as well as teas. Practically next door is **Queenz Grill Bar Deli** (Havelská 12, Staré Město, tel. 02/ 206–095), with take-out Greek salads and falafel, genuine hummus, and baba ghannouge. The bakeries at the **Krone** and **Kotva** department stores *(see above)* sell surprisingly delicious breads and pastries. Both stores also have large, well-stocked basement grocery stores.

Fun Things for Children Children enjoy the beautiful watercolor and colored-chalk sets available in nearly every stationery store at rock-bottom prices. The Czechs are also master illustrators, and the books they've made for young "pre-readers" are some of the world's loveliest. The best store to browse in is **Albatros** (Na perštýně 1, tel. 02/2422–3227), on the corner with Národní třída. They carry a large selection of children's books as well as cuddly stuffed animals, and they've created a fun play area for young customers. Many stores also offer unique wooden toys. For these, look in at **Obchod Vším Možným** (Nerudova 45, tel. 02/536941). For older children and teens, it's worth considering a Czech or Eastern European watch, telescope, or set of binoculars. The quality/price ratio is unbeatable.

Jewelry The **Granát** shop at Dlouhá 28 in the Old Town has a comprehensive selection of garnet jewelry, plus contemporary and traditional pieces set in gold and silver. Several shops specializing in gold jewelry line Wenceslas Square.

High Fashion Prague may not be Paris or Milan when it comes to fashion, but it is making a valiant effort to catch up. Playful designs in silky fabrics can be found at **Modes Robes** (Benediktská 5, tel. 02/232–2461). **A+G Flora** (Rytířská 31, tel. 02/2423–0614) is a showcase for Prague designer Helena Fejková, who specializes in natural fabrics and dramatic shapes. **Modní Salon Nostalgie** (Jilská 22, tel. 02/266–256) is a *fin-de-siècle* studio full of elegant styles. The major cosmetics czars are making inroads in Prague: **Christian Dior** (Pařížská 7, tel. 02/232–6229 or 02/232–7382), **Elizabeth Arden** (Rybná 2, tel. 02/232–5471), **Estée Lauder** (Železná 18, tel. 02/2423–2023), and **Lancôme** (Jungmannovo nám. 20, tel. 02/2421–7189).

Musical Instruments One entertaining store with good bargains on new and used instruments is **Art Artelier 573** (Ovocný trh, tel. 02/2422–0926). The staff is happy to test anything that catches your eye. Specializing in sheet music, **Capriccio** (Újezd 15, tel. 02/532–507) may well have the biggest selection in the country, with everything from jazz to classical to Broadway musicals.

Sports Equipment All Prague department stores carry middling-quality equipment from time to time. Your best bets for top-rate skis, skates, tennis racquets, or whatever else you forgot to bring is **Adidas** (Na příkopě 8, tel. 02/2421–0528). **Sports YMCA** (Na poříčí 12, tel. 02/232–3963) is the place to buy sleeping bags and backpacks. **VHV/Opus** (Vodičkova 7, tel. 02/203–628) stocks backpacks and equipment.

4 Dining

Dining possibilities in Prague have increased greatly in the past year as hundreds of new places have opened to cope with the increased tourist demand. Quality and price can vary widely, though. Be wary of tourist traps; cross-check prices of foreign-language menus with Czech versions. Also ask if there is a *denní lístek* (daily menu). These menus, usually written only in Czech, generally list cheaper and often fresher selections. Note that many places provide daily menus only for the midday meal.

The crush of visitors has placed tremendous strain on the more popular restaurants. The upshot is that reservations are nearly always required; this is especially true during peak tourist periods. If you don't have reservations, try arriving a little before standard meal times: 11:30 AM for lunch, or 5:30 PM for dinner.

A cheaper and quicker alternative to the sit-down establishments listed below would be to take a light meal at one of the city's growing number of street stands and fast-food places. Look for stands offering *párek* (hot dogs) or *smažený sýr* (fried cheese). McDonald's, with several locations in the city, has been joined by other fast-food imports from the West like Pizza Hut, Kentucky Fried Chicken, and Hardee's. For more exotic fare, try a gyro (made from pork) at the stand on the Staroměstské náměstí or the very good vegetarian fare at **Country Life** (Melantrichova 15, Staré Město, tel. 02/2421–3366; Jungmannova 1, Nové Město, tel. 02/2419–1739). The German coffeemaker Tchibo has teamed up with a local bakery and now offers tasty sandwiches and excellent coffee at convenient locations on the Staroměstské náměstí and at the top of Wenceslas Square.

Highly recommended restaurants in each price category are indicated by a star ★.

$$$$ **Hanavský Pavilon.** On a warm summer night there may be no more romantic spot in Prague than the terrace of this mock-Baroque fantasy pavilion high above the river. The appetizers are only adequate but lead to worthy main courses such as pork tenderloin with green-pepper sauce and stuffed quail. Vegetable side dishes are cooked properly, still an uncommon

feat in Prague. *Letenské sady 173, Prague 7, tel. 02/325-792. Reservations required for dinner. Jacket and tie advised. AE, MC, V.*

$$$$ Parnas. This is the first choice for visiting dignitaries and businesspeople blessed with expense accounts. Creative, freshly prepared cuisine, more nouvelle than Bohemian, is served in an opulent 1920s setting. Window seats afford stunning views of Prague Castle. Parnas has a small, mostly Czech vintage wine list and a fine selection of appetizers and desserts (the chocolate mousse is a must). *Smetanovo nábřeží 2, Nove Město, tel. 02/2422-7614. Reservations advised. Jacket and tie required. AE, MC, V.*

$$$$ Praha Tamura. Serving sushi and sashimi that's ★ extraordinarily fresh for a landlocked country, this restaurant has all the authentic Japanese touches you'd expect, such as a black-and-white minimalist decor and bonsai trees. Try *sashimi moriawase*, a mouth-watering sampler of delicate salmon, tuna, and squid pieces. Other classics include tempura and *soba* (buckwheat) noodles. Meals are available à la carte or fixed-price. *Havelská 6, Prague 1, tel. 02/2423-2056. Reservations advised. Jacket and tie advised. AE, MC, DC.*

$$$$ Rhapsody Piano Bar. Flickering candles on the tables and live music create an aura of romance at this comfortable restaurant that emphasizes French and Middle Eastern dishes. The service is multilingual and pleasant. Rhapsody's most popular main courses include chicken *shish taouk:* marinated chicken with a light accent of thyme and garlic. Steaks are satisfying, and fresh salmon with pink-pepper sauce is a treat. The best desserts are French: delicate crème brûlée and chocolate mousse. *Dukelských hrdinů, Prague 7, tel. 02/806-768. Reservations advised. Jacket and tie advised. AE, MC, V.*

$$$$ U modré kachničky. The "Blue Duck" sports ★ bright-blue paint on the outside and the city's most beautiful dining room inside—try for a seat at the back, where the walls are covered with stunning murals. The appetizers, such as goose liver on toast, are generally excellent. The well-thought-out entrées reflect several national cuisines; wild game is a specialty in autumn. Don't skip the apple strudel. *Nebovidská 6, Malá Strana, tel. 02/539-751. Reservations re-*

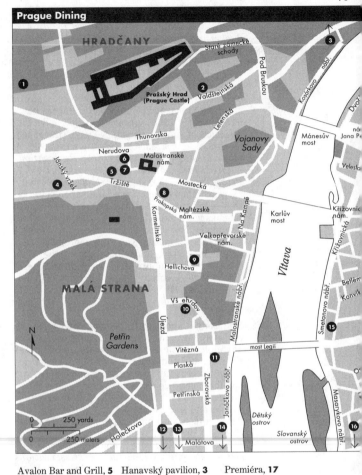

Prague Dining

HRADČANY

Staré zámecké schody

Pražský Hrad
(Prague Castle)

Valdštejnská

Pod Bruskou

Košťákovo nábř.

Dvoř

Mánesův
most

nábř.
Jana Pe

Velesla

Thunovska

Nerudova

Malostranské
nám.

Letenská

Vojanovy
Sady

Jánský vršek

Tržiště

Mostecká

Prokopská Maltézské
nám.

Na Kampě

Karlův
most

Křižovnic
nám.

Křižovnická

Karmelitská

Velkopřevorské
nám.

Hellichova

Betlém

Konvik

MALÁ STRANA

Vltava

Malostranské nábř.

Smetanovo nábř.

Vš ehrdov

Petřín
Gardens

N

Vítězná

most Legii

Plaská

Petřínská

Zborovská

Janáčkovo nábř.

Dětský
ostrov

Masarykovo nábř.

0   250 yards
0   250 meters

Holečkova

Malátova

Slovanský
ostrov

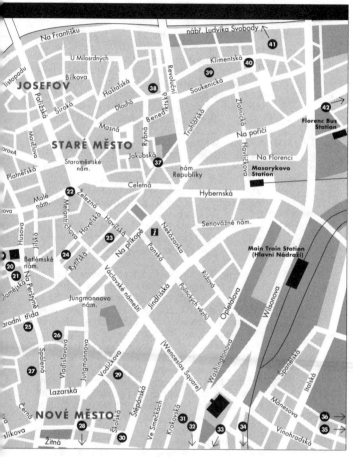

quired for dinner. Jacket and tie advised. No credit cards.

\$\$\$\$ **U Zlaté Hrušky.** At this bustling bistro perched on one of Prague's prettiest cobblestone streets, slide into one of the cozy dark-wood booths and let the cheerful staff advise on wines and specials. Duck and carp are house favorites. After dinner, stroll to the castle for an unforgettable panorama. *Nový Svět 3, Hradčany, tel. 02/531133. Reservations required. Jacket and tie advised. AE, DC, MC, V.*

\$\$\$\$ **V Zátiší.** White walls and casual grace accentuate the subtle flavors of smoked salmon, plaice, beef Wellington, and other non-Czech specialties. Order the house *Rulandské červené*, a fruity Moravian red wine that meets the exacting standards of the food. In behavior unusual for the city, the benign waiters fairly fall over each other to serve diners. *Liliová 1, Betlémské nám., Staré Město, tel. 02/2422–8977. Reservations advised. Dress: casual but neat. AE, MC, V.*

★

\$\$\$ **Cerberus.** Traditional Czech cooking is raised to an uncommonly high level at this New Town restaurant. The Bohemian staples of pork, duck, rabbit, and game are prepared and presented (by an attentive staff) as haute cuisine. Despite the modern decor, the ambience is warm and intimate. *Soukenická 19, Nové Město, tel. 02/231–0985 or 02/231–6777. Reservations advised. Dress: casual but neat. AE, MC, V.*

\$\$\$ **Fakhreldine.** This elegant Lebanese restaurant, crowded with diplomats who know where to find the real thing, has an excellent range of Middle Eastern appetizers and main courses. For a moderately priced meal, try several appetizers—hummus and garlic yogurt, perhaps—instead of a main course. *Klimentská 48, Prague 1, tel. 02/232–7970. Reservations advised. Dress: casual but neat. AE, DC, MC, V.*

\$\$\$ **Lobkovická.** This dignified *vinárna* (wine hall) set inside a 17th-century town palace serves some of Prague's most imaginative dishes. Chicken breast with crabmeat and curry sauce is an excellent main dish and typical of the kitchen's innovative approach to sauces and spice. Deep-red carpeting sets the perfect mood for enjoying bottles of Moravian wine brought from the musty depths of the restaurant's wine cel-

★

lar. *Vlašská 17, Malá Strana, tel. 02/530185. Reservations advised. Jacket and tie required. AE, MC, V.*

$$$ Premiéra. This is the place to go for a dress-up fish dinner. Elegantly set tables are spaced so guests can't eavesdrop on each other as they dine on salmon, shark, and other selections of whatever's fresh that day. *V jirchářích 6, Nové Město, tel. 02/2491–5672. Reservations advised. Jacket and tie advised. AE, DC, MC, V.*

$$$ U Mecenáše. ★ A fetching Renaissance inn from the 17th century, with dark, high-backed benches in the front room and cozy, elegant sofas and chairs in back, this is the place to splurge: From the aperitifs to the steaks and the cognac (swirled lovingly in oversize glasses), the presentation is seamless. *Malostranské nám. 10, Malá Strana, tel. 02/533881. Reservations advised. Jacket and tie required. AE, DC, MC, V. No lunch.*

$$$ U modré růže. The small "Blue Rose" can feel cozy or cramped, depending on your taste or your feelings about your dining partner, but starters such as the divine tagliatelli with smoked salmon and Parmesan will focus your attention on the meal. Fillet of lamb with shallots and caramel, and aubergine Provençal are also terrific, and entrées such as ostrich steak and "Dundee" alligator steak pique your interest if not necessarily your appetite. There is a full array of wines but a somewhat disappointing dessert selection. *Rytířská 16, Staré Město, tel. 02/261–081. Reservations advised. Jacket and tie advised. AE, DC, MC, V.*

$$ Avalon Bar and Grill. ★ This is a pleasant place for a late dinner after a concert at nearby St. Nicholas Cathedral or Lichtenstein Palace or after a taxing day of sightseeing at Prague Castle. Sink into comfortable wicker chairs and dig into the delicious pesto bread starter, or go for a hearty chicken sandwich or curried tofu. Lentil soup with cream is especially good, as are the onion rings and cheeseburgers. The tempting, varied menu, presented on the table as a placemat, has more than enough to satisfy vegetarians and carnivores alike. *Malostranské nám. 12, Malá Strana, tel. 02/530–276 or 02/530–263. Reservations not necessary. Dress: casual but neat. MC, V.*

\$\$ **Bella Napoli.** Come here for real Italian food at a
★ price/quality ratio that's hard to beat in Prague.
Ignore the faux-Italian interior and the alabas-
ter Venus de Milos astride shopping-mall foun-
tains and head straight for the 65-Kč. antipasto
bar, which will distract you with fresh olives,
eggplant, squid, and mozzarella. For your main
course, go with any of a dozen superb pasta
dishes or splurge with shrimp or chicken parmi-
giana. *V jámě 8, Nové Město, tel. 02/2422–7315.
Reservations advised. Dress: casual. No credit
cards.*

\$\$ **Café Savoy.** A large, well-proportioned room
with a splendid, restrained, yet exuberant ceiling restored to its 1887 appearance, the Savoy
needs only better-chosen furniture and better-
than-average coffee to grow into a superb coffee
house. Grilled meats and salad can make a light
meal, but most guests come for coffee or drinks.
The National Theater is just across the river,
making this a good place to come after the ballet
or opera. *Vítězná 5, Prague 5, tel. 02/539–796.
Reservations advised. Dress: casual but neat.
AE, DC, MC, V.*

\$\$ **Dolly Bell.** Tantalizing Yugoslav specialties in a
★ stylishly weird decor (with upside-down tables
hanging from the ceiling) keep this place busy.
The name comes from the title of a famous Yugoslav film. A sampling of appetizers—from corn-
bread filled with *proja* (Balkan cheese) to
gibanica (cheese pie)—can be a meal in itself.
Most of the main courses are meaty: *čevapčiči*
(pork sausage) is good, and the desserts, such as
baked apple *tufahija* (with a sticky, nutty filling) are heavenly. It's a short walk from the
tram stop Výtoň (Trams 3, 7, and 17).
*Neklanova 20, Prague 2, tel. 02/298–815. Reser-
vations advised. Dress: casual but neat. AE.*

\$\$ **Gany's.** Popular with the after-theater crowd in
the evening as well as throughout the day, this
big, bright restaurant with an excellent view of
Národní třída (National Avenue) has something
for everyone. Vegetarians are satisfied with yo-
gurt soup, vegetables with curry sauce, and
fresh salads and spaghetti; diners looking for
something meatier enjoy English roast beef and
Czech goulash or Russian crab with spicy sauce.
The beer is Radegast 12°. There is a full array of

coffees and scrumptious chocolate desserts. *Národní třída 20, Prague 1, tel. 02/297–665. Reservations not necessary. Dress: casual but neat. No credit cards.*

\$\$ Myslivna. The name means "hunting lodge," and the cooks at this far-flung neighborhood eatery certainly know their way around venison, quail, and boar. Attentive staff can advise on wines: Try Vavřinecké, a hearty red that holds its own with any beast. The stuffed quail and the leg of venison with walnuts both get high marks. A cab from the city center to Myslivna should cost under 200 Kč. *Jagellonská 21, Prague 3, tel. 02/6270209. Reservations advised. Dress: casual but neat. AE, V.*

\$\$ Palffy palác. The faded cream-and-white elegance of this restaurant hidden in the heart of a Baroque palace evokes centuries of history, but the menu modernizes Czech standards such as fried pork, fried cheese, and trout, all handled with a light touch. The small selection of salads is quite good. The view from the terrace ranks with the best. *Valdštejnská 14, Malá Strana, tel. 02/513–2418. Reservations advised. Dress: casual but neat. AE, MC, V.*

\$\$ Penguin's. The emphasis at this popular eatery is on classic Czech and international dishes, served in an elegant mauve-and-matte-black setting. Try any of the steaks or the chicken breast with potatoes. The penguin in the name refers to the Pittsburgh variety, of hockey fame—the owner's favorite team. *Zborovská 5, Prague 5, tel. 02/545660. Reservations advised. Dress: casual but neat. AE, MC, V.*

\$\$ Pezinok. Slovak cooking is hard to find in Prague, and this cozy wine restaurant is still the best in town. Heavy furnishings and subdued lighting add an oddly formal touch. Order à la carte (the set menus are overpriced) and choose from homemade sausages or *halušky*, boiled noodles served with a tangy sheep's cheese. The restaurant's full-bodied wines come from the Slovak town for which the restaurant was named. *Purkyňova 4, Nové Město, tel. 02/291996. Reservations advised. Dress: casual but neat. AE, MC, V.*

\$\$ Red Hot and Blues. You may think you're in a laid-back joint in New Orleans. This has all the best Creole hits, such as shrimp étoufée, lime-spiked grilled chicken breasts, and spicy soups, as well as a few Tex-Mex favorites like burritos. Weekend brunches are terrific; weekday nights often feature live jazz. *Jakubská 12, Prague 1, tel. 02/231–4639. Reservations not necessary. Dress: casual. AE, MC, V.*

$$ U Betlémské kaple. You'll know the specialty is fish from the lively carvings on the massive wooden benches at this pub-restaurant. The standbys, carp and trout, are here, joined by lesser-met domestic fish such as eel and pike. There's good Pilsener beer on tap. *Betlémské nám. 2, Staré Město, tel. 02/2421–1879. Reservations not necessary. Dress: casual but neat. AE, DC, MC, V.*

$$ U Čížků. Although it's no secret to herds of
★ tour-bus travelers, this large, borderline-elegant restaurant is nonetheless an excellent spot in which to savor authentic Czech cooking at its best. Especially recommended are the beef in citrony cream sauce (*svíčková*), and roast duck and goose. Be sure to save room for fruit dumplings, apple strudel, or *lívanečky* (little pancakes topped with cranberries and whipped cream). The service is pleasant and obliging. *Karlovo nám. 34, Nové Město, tel. 02/298–891. Reservations required. Dress: casual but neat. AE, MC.*

$$ U maltézských rytířů. The tongue-twisting name means "Knights of Malta," a reference to the Catholic knightly order whose embassy is nearby. Ask for a table in the ancient cellar; upstairs it's less formal but less spacious. The short menu offers two reliable regulars: Prokopius beefsteak, stuffed with almonds, and Old Prague pork fillet. The service is friendly and attentive. *Prokopská 10, Malá Strana, tel. 02/536–357. Reservations advised. Dress: casual but neat. AE, MC, V.*

$$ U Mikulaše Dačického. Escape the uninspiring landscape of Smíchov by ducking into this cozy wine restaurant whose walls depict boisterous scenes of Renaissance life. The servings of standard beef, pork, and trout are huge; if none of that appeals, try curry chicken. *Victora Huga 2, Prague 5, tel. 02/549–312. Reservations advised. Dress: casual but neat. No credit cards. No lunch.*

$$ **U Pastýřky.** This backwoods-cabin–style Slovak restaurant (the name means "the shepherdess") is well worth the tram journey from the center of Prague. Long tables with benches easily accommodate the crowds of locals and tourists alike who flock here to savor the succulent chicken and steak cooked on a grill in the middle of the restaurant, as well as the abundant selection of Slovak wines. Also recommended are cabbage soup and pasta appetizers. A cover charge may be tacked on your bill. *Bělehradská 15, Prague 4, tel. 02/434–093. Reservations advised. Dress: casual but neat. AE, MC, V.*

$ ★ **Bar Bar.** Cheap and delicious, the food at Bar Bar is international with a French accent. Try the *croque monsieur* or crepe specialties with names like Bretagne and Normandy. Fillings for crepes may include ham, four kinds of cheese, and apples or jam. The crepes, while scrumptious, are a bit small; it's best to order a big salad on the side—or another crepe for dessert. The black padded door at street level may look off-putting, but the restaurant below is large, with bright white walls and plenty of elbow room. *Všehrdova 17, Malá Strana, no phone. Reservations not necessary. Dress: casual. MC.*

$ **Café Milena.** Milena Jesenská today is mainly known as one of Franz Kafka's lovers and the recipient of letters published as his book *Letters to Milena,* but in her day she was also a prominent Prague journalist and intellectual. This fairly new café with its Art Nouveau furnishings and atmosphere is named after her. Café Milena's coffees, pastries, and ice cream are excellent, and the view over Old Town Square is even better. *Staroměstské nám. 22, Old Town Sq., tel. 02/260–843. Reservations not necessary. Dress: casual but neat. No credit cards.*

$ ★ **Demínka.** This spacious 19th-century café offers some respite from Prague's throngs of tourists. It's a perfect place to have coffee and write a letter. Try the cheap and tasty *Smažený sýr* (fried cheese) or the hearty goulash soup. A small sandwich or schnitzel at Demínka makes a fine afternoon snack. *Škrétova 1, Prague 2, tel. 02/2422–3383. Reservations not necessary. Dress: casual but neat. MC, V.*

$ Na Zvonařce. This bright beer hall supplements traditional Czech dishes—mostly pork, beer, and pork—with some innovative Czech and international choices, all at unbeatably cheap prices. Noteworthy entrées include juicy fried chicken and English roast beef; fruit dumplings for dessert are a rare treat. The service may be slow, but that simply allows time to commune with a tankard of ale on the outside terrace during the summer. *Šafaříkova 1, Prague 2, tel. 02/ 254–534. Reservations advised. No credit cards.*

$ Pizzeria Kmotra. Packed almost all the time, the "Godfather's" pizzas, especially the tasty four-cheese version, are worth the wait. The café upstairs leads to the restaurant in an ancient cellar downstairs, with its sturdy, long wooden tables and benches. *V jirchářích 12, Nové Město, no phone. Reservations not necessary. Dress: casual but neat. No credit cards.*

$ Profit. The unfortunate name masks a clean, spacious pub that serves such excellent Czech standbys as goulash and pork with dumplings and sauerkraut at astonishingly reasonable prices. The central location could hardly be better. *Betlémské nám. 8, Staré Město, tel. 02/ 2422–2776. Reservations not necessary. No credit cards.*

$ Symphony. This well-run place spiffs up an old Czech idea—the cheap *jídelna,* or cafeteria—with cool gray-and-white décor and prints and posters with a musical motif appropriate to this site in the Academy of Music. The goulash, vegetarian, and roast specials change daily; salads, sandwiches, and desserts, including rarely seen muffins, suffice for a snack or light meal. *Lichtenstein Palace, Malostranské nám. 13, Malá Strana, no phone. Reservations not necessary. Dress: casual but neat. No credit cards.*

$ U Govindy. Enter with a beatific disposition or at least an open mind. This small restaurant run by the local Hare Krishnas and open only from noon to 6 PM serves one vegetarian meal (which varies daily) composed of fresh whole grains, vegetables, soup, a sweet drink and dessert. Donations of 25 Kč and up are requested. Share a table downstairs or sit on the floor (after first removing your shoes) in the tiny upstairs loft. *Na hrazi, Prague 8, near metro Palmovka, no phone. Res-*

ervations not necessary. Dress: casual. No credit cards.

$ **U Koleje.** This laid-back pub is suitable for the
★ entire family. Besides offering excellent beers,
U Koleje serves pork and beef dishes. During
peak hours you may have to share a table.
Slavíkova 24, Prague 2, tel. 02/627–4163. Reservations advised. No credit cards.

$ **U Matouše.** Nothing special here in the way of
★ decoration—except for its being cleaner than
most pubs—but the food attracts devoted followers. Traditional fare like Moravian pork or
roast duck is handled with aplomb. Just as successful are such exotic dishes as chicken in
curry-yogurt sauce. *Preslova 17, Prague 5, tel.
02/546–284. Reservations not necessary. Dress:
casual. No credit cards.*

$ **U Šumavy.** The traditional Czech cooking at this
pub is popular with people who study at the
French Institute down the block. The front
room can be smoky; the back room is quieter and
easier on the lungs. Pork with dumplings and
sauerkraut is tasty. *Štěpánská 3, Nové Město,
tel. 02/294–194. Reservations not necessary.
Dress: casual. No credit cards.*

$ **V Dlouhé.** Here you'll find good, solid—but not
heavy—Bohemian cooking served in a wood-
furnished room. There is also a good selection of
dishes, including rabbit or carp in sweet black
sauce, and *stíka* (pike). *Dlouhá 35, Staré Město,
tel. 02/231–6125. Reservations advised. Dress:
casual. AE, MC, V.*

$ **Velryba.** A fixture among the arty crowd (local
and expatriate), this café-gallery-pub is thick
with the smoke and roaring conversation of authentic Czech gathering places. Good, filling,
cheap, pub food such as fried cheese and fried
fish, plus pasta dishes (more Czech than Italian)
keep appetites satisfied while liquors of all varieties keep the talk flowing. *Opatovická 24, Nové
Město, tel. 2491–2391. Reservations not necessary. Dress: casual. No credit cards.*

$ **V Krakovské.** At this clean, proper pub that is
close to the major tourist sights, the food is traditional and hearty; this is the place to try Bohemian duck, washed down with a dark beer from
Domažlice in western Bohemia. *Krakovská 20,
Nové Město, tel. 02/261537. Reservations not
necessary. Dress: casual. No credit cards.*

5 Lodging

Since 1989, visitors have been less and less disappointed by the city's lodging, now that more hotels are being built and renovated. Most hotels, particularly in the city center, have managed to raise their facilities (as well as their prices) to Western standards. In most of the very expensive and expensive hotels (designated by four and three stars, respectively, *below*), you can expect to find a restaurant and an exchange bureau on or near the premises, as well as a color TV and a minibar in your room. Bills are paid in crowns, although some hotels may accept payment in hard (that is, Western) currency. During summer, reservations are imperative.

A cheaper and often more interesting alternative to Prague's generally expensive hotels are private rooms and apartments. The city is full of travel agencies offering such accommodations; the only drawback is that you may have to sacrifice a little privacy. The best, most prominent room-finding service is **AVE**. Prices start at about $15 per person per night. Insist on a room in the city center if you don't want to find yourself in a dreary, far-flung suburb. AVE has offices at several locations throughout the city: at the main train station (Hlavní nádraží, tel. 02/2422–3226, open daily 6 AM–11:30 PM), at Holešovice train station (Nádraží Holešovice, open daily 6:15 AM–11 PM), the airport (Letiště Ruzyně, open daily 7 AM–11:30 PM), in Nové Město (Panská 4, open weekdays 8:30–6, weekends 8:30–4), and on Old Town Square (Staroměstské nám. 24, open weekdays 8:30–7, weekends 9–6).

Another helpful agency is **Stop City** (Vinohradská 24, Prague 2, tel. 02/2423–1233, tel and fax 02/2422–2497; open fall–spring, daily 11–8; summer, daily 10–9). Prices start at about $12 per person per night for a room in an apartment; self-service private apartments start from about $20 per person; rooms in pensions run from about $30 per person. Most of Stop City's accommodations are clustered in the city center. Other helpful room-finding agencies include **Hello Ltd.** (Senovážné nám. 3, Nové Město, tel. 02/2421–4212, open daily 9 AM–10 PM), **City of Prague Accommodation Service** (Haštalské nám.

8, tel. 02/2481–0603, open daily 9 AM–8 PM), and **Prague Suites Accommodation Service** (Melantrichova 8, Staré Město, tel. 02/2422–9961, fax 02/2422–9363, open weekdays 9–6, Sat. 9–2).

Highly recommended lodgings in each price category are indicated by a star ★.

$$$$ **Diplomat.** This sprawling complex opened in
★ 1990 and is still regarded as the best business hotel in town. Even though it's in the suburbs, the Diplomat is convenient to the airport and, via the metro, to the city center. The modern rooms may not exude much character, but they are tastefully furnished and quite comfortable. The hotel staff are competent and many are bilingual. Guests have access to a pool, sauna, and fitness center. *Evropská 15, Prague 6, tel. 02/ 2439–4111, fax 02/2439–4215. 387 rooms with bath. Facilities: restaurant, bar, nightclub, pool, fitness center, sauna, conference room. AE, DC, MC, V.*

$$$$ **Forum Praha.** A skyscraper that juts out of the relatively smooth skyline of Prague, this hotel is considered an eyesore by many citizens. Rooms at the Forum nonetheless offer the hotel guest a magnificent view of Prague, particularly if you're lucky enough to get a room facing the Prague Castle. The Forum is sleek and modern in every respect; rooms are spacious, and all of the expected amenities are in place. Many rooms are designated for nonsmokers only. The Vyšehrad subway station is just a few steps from the hotel; it's only five minutes to the city center. *Kongresová 1, Prague 4, tel. 02/6119– 1111 or 02/6126–1673, fax 02/420–684. 531 rooms with bath. Facilities: restaurants, café, nightclub, bowling alley, pool, fitness center. AE, MC, DC, V.*

$$$$ **Grand Hotel Bohemia.** This beautifully refurbished Art Nouveau town palace is just a stone's throw from the Old Town Square. The new Austrian owners opted for a muted, modern decor in the rooms but left the sumptuous public areas just as they were. Each room is outfitted with fax and answering machine. *Králodvorska 4, Staré Město, tel. 02/232–3417), fax 02/232–9545. 78 rooms with bath. Facilities: restaurant, café. AE, DC, MC, V.*

$$$$ **Hoffmeister.** Infused with a friendly elegance
★ and an atmosphere unlike that of any other hotel
in the city, the Hoffmeister occupies a choice
corner, with the castle looming above Malá
Strana and the river stretching out below. The
standard double rooms are a bit small, but each
is decorated with an eye for style, not just luxury, and good prints and collages by Adolf
Hoffmeister, father of the present owner, hang
in every room. The restaurant sends dishes up
to the castle for state dinners, and the wine cellar is small but discriminating. *Pod Bruskou 9,
Malá Strana, tel. 02/538–380, fax 02/530–959.
38 rooms with bath. Facilities: restaurant, bar,
garage. AE, DC, MC, V.*

$$$$ **Palace.** For the well-heeled, this is Prague's
most coveted address—an art-nouveau town
palace perched on a busy corner only a block
from the very central Wenceslas Square. Renovated in 1989, the hotel's spacious, well-appointed rooms, each with a private white
marble bathroom, are fitted in velvety pinks and
greens cribbed straight from an Alfons Mucha
print. Two rooms are set aside for disabled travelers. The ground-floor buffet boasts the city's
finest salad bar. *Panská 12, Nové Město, tel. 02/
2409–3111, fax 02/2422–1240. 125 rooms with
bath. Facilities: 2 restaurants, café, bar, snack
bar, satellite TV, minibars. AE, DC, MC, V.*

$$$$ **Paříž.** The smallish rooms hardly justify the
high price, yet the hotel's unique Art Nouveau
facade and its excellent location near the Old
Town's Powder Tower keep the occupancy rate
near 99%. Ask for a room away from the decep-
tively peaceful street. The coffeehouse on the
ground floor is one of the city's most elegant. *U
Obecního domů 1, Staré Město, tel. 02/2422–
2151, fax 02/2422–5475. 100 rooms with bath.
Facilities: restaurant, café. AE, DC, MC, V.*

$$$$ **Pension U Raka.** This private guest house offers
★ the peace and coziness of an alpine lodge, plus a
quiet location on the ancient, winding streets of
Nový Svět, just behind the Loretan Church and
a 10-minute walk from Prague Castle. The dark
wood building has only five rooms, but if you can
get a reservation (try at least a month in advance), you will gain a wonderful base for ex-
ploring Prague. *Černínská ul. 10/93, tel. 02/*

Prague Lodging

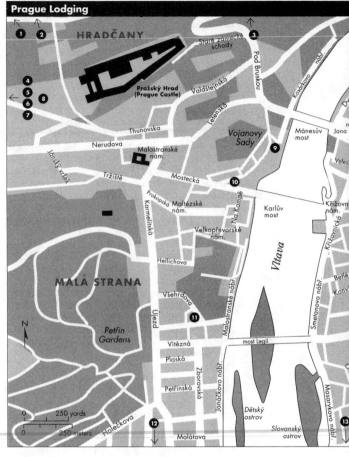

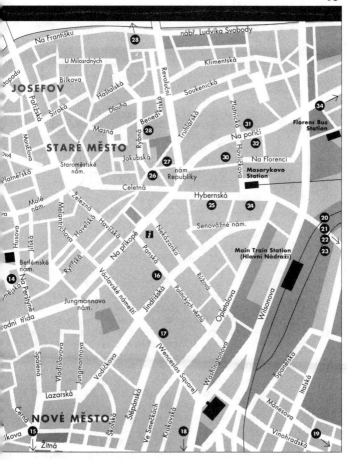

351453, fax 02/353074. 5 rooms with bath. AE, DC, V.

$$$$ Praha. A gigantic pile looming over the Dejvice district, the Praha's size and style, or lack of style, epitomize the inflated self-image and paranoia of the communist ruling elite before 1989. They built the place, completely fenced in with only one access point, to house visiting dignitaries and party officials. Open to the public since 1990, it offers more than overgrown kitsch: magnificent views from every one of the large rooms (which have furnishings that would be quite comfortable in a vacation cottage) and rates that are at the lower end of the $$$$ price category. *Sušická 20, Prague 6, tel. 02/2434–1111, fax 02/2431–1218. 14 rooms with bath. Facilities: restaurant, lounge, fitness center, bowling alley, tennis courts, secretarial service, garage. AE, DC, MC, V.*

$$$$ Renaissance. Still gleaming with its gray-blue facade and stained-glass murals, this large hotel across from the Masarykovo train station has made a concerted effort to attract business travelers. Its location is excellent for quick access to highways, New Town offices, or Old Town restaurants. Tourists have a better chance of getting a room in June and July, slow months for conferences and trade shows. As in most newer hotels in Prague, the rooms are on the sterile side but lack nothing in the way of creature comforts, and some have wonderful views of Old Town rooftops. *V celnici 7, Nové Město, tel. 02/2481–0396, fax 02/231–3133. 309 rooms with bath. Facilities: 2 restaurants, 3 wheelchair-accessible rooms, non-smoking floor, conference rooms, fitness center. AE, DC, MC, V.*

$$$ Atrium Praha. The rooms may be a bit small, but the boxy center atrium is enormous and impressive, a veritable glass city, with noiseless glass elevators and gently bubbling fountains. Ask for a room facing the river or Old Town. The gorgeous swimming pool is almost never busy. The Atrium Praha is a five-minute walk from the subway, although the first part of the route involves walking along a rather desolate, depressing block. *Pobřežní 1, Prague 8, tel. 02/2484–1111, fax 02/2481–1973. 788 rooms with bath. Facilities: restaurants, café, bar, pool, fitness* center, salon, conference halls. AE, MC, DC, V.

$$$ Betlem Club. This pension hovers on the margin between the $$$ and $$ price categories, offering well-appointed rooms, a cozy Romanesque cellar breakfast room, and a favorable location on one of the Old Town's most picturesque squares. Some of the rooms are good-size, some are decorated with black-lacquer furniture, and all have a television and telephone. *Betlémské nám. 9, Staré Město, tel. 02/2421–6872, fax 02/ 2421–8054. 20 rooms with bath. Cash only.*

$$$ City Hotel Moráň. This 19th-century town house was tastefully renovated in 1992; now the lobby and public areas are bright and inviting, made over in an updated Jugendstil style. The modern if slightly bland rooms are a cut above the Prague standard for convenience and cleanliness; ask for one on the sixth floor for a good view of Prague Castle. A hearty Sunday brunch is served in the ground-floor restaurant. *Na Moráni 15, Prague 2, tel. 02/2491–5208, fax 02/ 297533. 57 rooms, most with bath. Facilities: restaurant, bar. AE, DC, MC, V.*

$$$ Evropa. "Faded elegance" is the catch phrase here. The exterior of this hotel is so beautiful, with its Art Nouveau flourishes and mosaics, that travelers may not mind so much that lobby lights are a bit too wan and many of the rooms look forlorn. (Rooms without bath are cheaper.) The hotel dates from 1889 (Art Nouveau touches were added 1903–1905), but most of the period furniture has been replaced by the socialist-issue style. Never mind: relax in the lovely street-level café, and pretend it's the 1920s. *Václavské nám. 25, Prague 1, tel. 02/2422–8117, fax 02/ 2422–4044. 87 rooms, 32 with bath. Facilities: restaurant, café. AE, DC, MC, V.*

$$$ Meteor Plaza. This popular Old Town hotel, operated by the Best Western chain, combines the best of New World convenience and Old World charm (Empress Maria Theresa's son, Joseph, stayed here when he was passing through in the 18th century). The setting is ideal: a newly renovated, Baroque building that is only five minutes by foot from downtown. There is a good, if touristy, in-house wine cellar. *Hybernská 6, Nové Město, tel. 02/2422–0664, fax 02/2421–*

3005. 86 rooms with bath. Facilities: restaurant, fitness center, garage. AE, DC, MC, V.

$$$ ★ U Páva. This newly renovated, neoclassical inn, set on a quiet gas-lit street in Malá Strana, offers upstairs suites that afford an unforgettable view of Prague Castle. Best of all, the U Páva is small and intimate—the perfect escape for those who've had their fill of cement high-rise resorts. The staff is courteous and helpful, while the reception and public areas are elegant and discreet. *U lužického semináře 22, Malá Strana, tel. 02/2451-0922, fax 02/533379. 11 rooms with bath. Facilities: restaurant, wine bar. AE, DC, MC, V.*

$$$ U Tří Pštrosů. The location could not be better—a romantic corner in the Malá Strana only a stone's throw from the river and the Charles Bridge. The airy rooms, dating back 300 years, still have their original oak-beamed ceilings and antique furniture; many also have views over the river. An excellent in-house restaurant serves traditional Czech dishes to guests and non-guests alike. *Dražického nám. 12, Malá Strana, tel. 02/2451-0779, fax 02/2451-0783. 18 rooms with bath. Facilities: restaurant. AE, MC, V.*

$$ Apollon. Situated on a tram line that leads directly into the center of Prague (a 10-minute ride without traffic), this simple, clean hotel has adequate rooms, each equipped with color television and satellite hookup. The neighborhood is safe but dull. It's easy access to the center that recommends this hotel. *Koněvova 158, Prague 3, tel. 02/644-2414, fax 02/644-2430. 50 rooms with bath. Facilities: restaurant. MC.*

$$ Ariston. The somewhat grimy, working-class neighborhood of Žižkov sprouts new, remodeled hotels faster than any other part of town. This one offers acceptable comfort and facilities with good connections to the city center. The main train station is one tram stop away. The spotless rooms with television, telephone, minibar, and air-conditioning are pleasant, but try to get one away from the noisy street. *Seifertova 65, Prague 3, tel. 02/627-8840, fax 02/278-216. 58 rooms with bath. Facilities: restaurant, bar. AE, MC, V.*

$$ Axa. Funky and functional, this modernist high

rise, built in 1932, was a mainstay of the budget-hotel crowd until a recent reconstruction forced substantial price hikes. The rooms, now with color television sets and modern plumbing, are certainly improved; however, the lobby and public areas look decidedly tacky, with plastic flowers and glaring lights. *Na poříčí 40, tel. 02/ 2481–2580, fax 02/232–2172. 132 rooms, most with bath. Facilities: restaurant, bar, nightclub. AE, DC, MC, V.*

$$ Central. The name describes the best feature of this spartan establishment near Náměstí Republiky. It's probably the cheapest true hotel in the Old Town. The furnishings are functional, and rooms are clean; all have baths. Although the street itself could be anywhere, all the splendors of the Old Town—plus public transport and shopping—are seconds away. *Rybná 8, Staré Město, tel. 02/2481–2041, fax 02/232– 8404. 62 rooms with bath. Facilities: restaurant, nightclub. MC, V.*

$$ Fortuna. Named the Hotel Solidarita under communism, this large, boxy hotel has since undergone a complete face-lift, which included a peach-color paint job on the outside and the addition of a spiffy, large lobby that shimmers with the color mauve. Rooms are small but adequate. The hotel is far from the center in distance, but only five minutes by tram to the Želivského subway line, which whisks you into town. *Bečvářova 14, Prague 10, tel. 02/777–444, fax 02/777–441. 240 rooms with bath. Facilities: restaurant, bar, souvenir shop, beauty salon. AE, MC, V.*

$$ Harmony. This is one of the newly renovated, formerly state-owned standbys. The stern 1930s facade clashes with the bright, "nouveau riche" 1990s interior, but cheerful receptionists and big, clean rooms compensate for the aesthetic flaws. Ask for a room away from the bustle of one of Prague's busiest streets. *Na poříčí 31, tel. 02/232–0720, fax 02/231–0009. 60 rooms with bath. Facilities: restaurant, snack bar. AE, DC, MC, V.*

$$ Kampa. This early Baroque armory turned hotel
★ is tucked away on a leafy corner just south of Malá Strana. The rooms are clean, if sparse, though the bucolic setting makes up for any dis-

comforts. Note the late-Gothic vaulting in the massive dining room. *Všehrdova 16, Prague 1, tel. 02/2451–0409, fax 02/2451–0377. 85 rooms with bath. Facilities: restaurant, café. AE, DC, MC, V.*

$$ Karl-Inn. With a fresh coat of pink paint spiked with brown trim, Karl-Inn is a beacon of cheer in an otherwise down-at-the-heel neighborhood not far from the city center and five minutes from the Křižíkova metro station. The simple, basic rooms done in the simple, basic color of beige, have telephone and television. Each room also has a balcony, although the view is nothing special. The Karl-Inn is a good value for the money. *Šaldova 54, Prague 8, tel. 02/2481–1718, fax 02/2481–2681. 168 rooms with bath. Facilities: restaurant, conference rooms. AE, MC, V.*

$$ Mepro. Standard rooms and service and a reasonably central location make this small hotel worth considering. The Smíchov neighborhood offers a surprising range of dining options (try the excellent U Mikuláše Dačického wine restaurant across the street), nice strolls along the Vltava, and quick access to Malá Strana and the Petřín gardens. *Viktora Huga 3, Prague 5, tel. 02/561–8121, fax 02/527–343. 26 rooms with bath. Facilities: wine cellar. AE, MC, V.*

$$ Obora. If you don't mind being a half-hour from the center by public transport and enjoy greenery and history, think of this place. The large park adjacent—a good area for walking or jogging—saw fighting during the battle of Bílá Hora in 1620, which threw Protestant Bohemia forcibly back into the Catholic Hapsburg empire and fed the flames of central Europe's devastating Thirty Years' War. The hotel itself offers more modern but ordinary comforts. Book ahead, as it tends to fill up with French tour groups. *Libocká 271/1, Prague 6, tel. 02/367–779, fax 02/316–7125. 22 rooms with bath. Facilities: restaurant, bar. AE, DC, MC, V.*

$$ Opera. Once the hospice of choice for divas performing at the nearby State Theater, the Opera greatly declined under the Communists. New owners, however, are working hard to restore the hotel's former luster. Until then, the clean (but smallish) rooms, friendly staff, and fin-de-siècle charm are still reason enough to recommend it. *Těšnov 13, tel. 02/231–5609, fax 02/231–*

1477. 66 rooms, 26 with bath. Facilities: restaurant, snack bar. AE, DC, MC, V.

$$ Pension Větrník. Housed in a windmill dating from 1722 (the first in Prague, the proprietors will tell you), this small pension is imbued with a quality rarely found in Prague's hostelries: charm. Hefty wooden furnishings, the walled courtyard with its old well, and the friendly staff create a country-house air. The owner-chef will cook to your specifications. *U Větrníku 40–1, Prague 6, tel. 02/351–9622, fax 02/361–406. From airport, Bus 179 to Koleje Větrník stop. 6 rooms with bath. Facilities: tennis court, parking. MC.*

$$ Vítkov. Constructed on a semicircle over a major intersection in the working-class neighborhood of Žižkov, this hotel is similar in appeal to the Apollo (*see below*) and bigger in bulk, although not as modern. The rooms are clean and pleasant, decorated in red and brown. If street noise is a consideration, ask for a room in the back. *Koněvova 114, Prague 3, tel. 02/279–340, fax 02/279–357. 68 rooms with bath. Facilities: 2 restaurants, bar, café, conference rooms. AE, DC, MC, V.*

$ Apollo. This is a standard, no-frills, square-box hotel where clean rooms come at a fair price. Its primary flaw is its location, roughly 20 minutes by metro or bus from the city center. *Kubišova 23, tel. 02/6641–0628, fax 02/6641–4570. Metro Holešovice, then tram No. 5 or 17 to Hercovka. 35 rooms with bath or shower. AE, MC, V.*

$ Hybernia. The dull appearance of this train-station flophouse hardly suggests that it is actually a respectably clean, secure hotel. The rooms are of the two-bed-and-a-table variety but are perfectly adequate for short stays. The location, next to Masarykovo train station and a short walk from the main station, is excellent for the money. *Hybernská 24, tel. 02/2421–0439, fax 02/2421–1513. 80 rooms, some with bath. Facilities: restaurant, bar, lounge. No credit cards.*

$ Pension Digitals. This place offers excellent value for the money. The house lies about a 20-minute walk from the castle district, on a slightly funky street whose architecture brings to mind San Francisco's eclectic townhouses. Each of the spacious rooms has a television and telephone. *Na Petynce 106–143, Prague 6, tel. and* *fax 02/355–071. 10 rooms with bath. AE, DC, MC, V.*

$ Pension Janata. A little oasis on a crummy side street, this pension delights with its quiet, bright-white courtyard and pleasant service. Rooms are simple and clean; breakfast is included in the price. Exit this nook, and it's a few minutes to the tram, which heads straight into the city center or, in the other direction, to the Palmovka metro station. *Hájkova 19, Prague 3, tel. and fax 02/278–455. 7 rooms, 2 with bath. Facilities: restaurant, secure parking. AE, MC, V.*

$ Pension Větrný mlýn. This pleasant, bright pension is in the green western suburbs, near the airport and Route E48 from western Bohemia. Hvězda park, with its unusual Renaissance royal summer palace, rises above. Rooms are spare but comfortable, and breakfast is served on the premises. The restaurant at the Club Hotel Bohemia, across the street, serves local specialties. *Ruzyňská 3/96, Prague 6, tel. and fax 02/365–354. From airport, Bus 108 (weekday mornings only) to Ruzyňská škola stop. 10 rooms with bath. Cash only.*

6 The Arts and Nightlife

· Antonín Dvořák ·

The Arts

Prague's cultural flair is legendary, though performances are usually booked far in advance by all sorts of Praguers. The concierge at your hotel may be able to reserve tickets for you. Otherwise, for the cheapest tickets, go directly to the theater box office a few days in advance or immediately before a performance. **Bohemia Ticket International** (Na příkopě 16, tel. 02/2421–5031, and Václavské nám. 25, tel. 02/2422–7253) and **Tiketpro,** at several locations including Stěpánská 61, the Old Town Hall, and Národní 4 (central tel. 02/2423–2110, fax 02/2423–2021), sell tickets for major cultural events at semi-inflated prices. Tickets can also be purchased at **American Express** (*see* Staying in Prague in Chapter 1).

For details of cultural events, look to the English-language newspapers *The Prague Post* and *Prognosis*, or to the monthly English-language *Prague Guide*, available at hotels and tourist offices.

Film

If a film was made in the United States or Britain, the chances are good that it will be shown with Czech subtitles rather than dubbed. (Film titles, however, are usually translated into Czech, so your only clue to the movie's country of origin may be the poster used in advertisements.) Popular cinemas include **Blaník** (Václavské nám. 56, tel. 02/2421–6698), **Hvězda** (Václavské nám. 38, tel. 02/264545), **Paříž** (Václavské nám. 22, tel. 02/2422–0158), **U Hradeb 64** (Mostecká 21, tel. 02/535–006), and **Svetozor** (Vodičkova ul. 39, tel. 02/263616). Two film clubs showing classics and recent releases in their original languages are **Ponrepo** (Národní 40, tel. 02/2422–7137, inexpensive yearly membership required) and **Dlabačov** (Bělohorská 24, Prague 6, tel. 02/311–5328; tickets also sold at Tiketpro, Václavské nám. 38). Prague's English-language newspapers carry film reviews and full timetables.

Music

Classical concerts are held all over the city throughout the year. The excellent Czech Philharmonic has its home in **Dvořák Hall,** a small, ornate, slightly severe space with good acoustics (in Rudolfinum, nám. Jana Palacha, tel. 02/2489–3227). Until the resplendent Art Nouveau **Obecní dům** and its **Smetana Hall** reopen in 1997, the Prague Symphony Orchestra will also play in Dvořák Hall, as will the Czech Radio Orchestra, an ensemble noted for its skill with modern music. Performances also are held regularly in the **Lobkovicz Palace** at Prague Castle and in the gardens below the castle (where the music comes with a view). A handful of gorgeous churches and chapels host chamber performances. Among them are the two **Churches of St. Nicholas** (one is on Statoměstské nám., the other on Malostranské nám.), the **Church of Sts. Simon and Jude** on Dušní street near the Hotel Intercontinental, the **Zrcadlová kaple** (Mirror Chapel) in the Klementinum, and the part-Gothic, part-modern concert hall in the **Klášter sv. Anežky České** (St. Agnes Convent). Concerts at the **Villa Bertramka** (Mozartova 169, Smíchov, tel. 02/543893) emphasize the music of Mozart and his contemporaries (*see* Off the Beaten Track in Chapter 2). Performances combining the music of Dvořák with light drama based on the composer's life are given at the **Dvořák Museum** (Ke Karlovu 20, Prague 2, tel. 02/298–214), a charming villa.

Watch for concerts by the Prague Chamber Orchestra, the Talich Chamber Orchestra, and the Kocian or Wihan quartets for classical and romantic standards; the Prague Madrigalists or Ars Cameralis for medieval, Renaissance, and Baroque music played on period instruments; and the Agon ensemble for cutting-edge contemporary music.

Fans of organ music will be delighted by the number of recitals held in Prague's historic halls and churches. Popular programs are offered at **St. Vitus Cathedral** in Hradčany, **U Křížovníků** near the Charles Bridge, the **Church of St. Nicholas** in Malá Strana, and **St. James's Church** on Malá Štupartská in the Old Town, where the organ plays amid a complement of Baroque statuary.

The **Prague Spring Music Festival** brings top-quality ensembles and soloists to town for three weeks beginning in mid-May every year. The ticket office at Hellichova 18 in Malá Strana is open from mid-April through the festival's end.

Opera and Ballet

The Czech Republic has a strong operatic tradition, and performances at the **Národní divadlo** (National Theater, Národní třída 2, tel. 02/2491–3437) and the **Statní Opera Praha** (State Opera House, Wilsonova 4, tel. 02/265–353), at the top of Wenceslas Square, can be excellent. At the State Opera, a heavy diet of Verdi, Wagner, and other old-time favorites (sung in the original language) supports an occasional modern work, often of high merit. The National Theater presents many Czech operas, including perennial favorites like Smetana's *Bartered Bride* and Dvořák's *Rusalka*, as well as works by foreign composers. The historic **Stavovské divadlo** (Estates' Theater, Ovocný trh 1, Staré Město, tel. 02/2421–5001), where *Don Giovanni* debuted during the 18th century, specializes in Mozart's operas but also hosts straight drama. You're not likely to find a superstar tenor or soprano, except in rare solo recitals, but a stream of singers from Slovakia, Russia, Romania, and other points east keeps the overall standards quite high.

The National Theater's ballet corps concentrates on the bread-and-butter classics, although it sometimes ventures farther afield, choreographing subjects from modern drama and movies—even *Psycho*. The **Prague Chamber Ballet** handles its small repertoire of neoclassical dances with great style. Contemporary dance struggles for acceptance in Prague, notably through the annual **Tanec Praha** (Dance Prague) festival.

Theater

Most dramatic works are performed in Czech. For those who find the Czech language a vast mystery, try one of the many "black theater" houses. This Czech creation, nowadays a very expensive (by Czech standards) form of entertainment, is a melding of mime, visual effects, and film. Perhaps the most famous venue is the **Laterna Magika** (Národní třída 4, Nové Město, tel. 02/2491–4129). Tickets cost 450 Kč and sell out fast; the box office is open weekdays 10–8 and weekends 3–8. The long-running *Ahasver: Legends of Magic Prague* can be seen at **Černé divadlo Jiřího Srnce** (Black Theater of Jiří Srnec, the man credited with inventing the form, Národní 40, tel. 02/260–033). Another is **Divadlo Ta Fantastika** (Palác Unitaria, Karlova 8, tel. 02/2422–9078). Most dramatic performances at the Stavovské divadlo (*see* Opera and Ballet, *above*) are simultaneously translated into English through headsets. Several English-language theater groups operate sporadically in Prague; pick up a copy of *The Prague Post* or *Prognosis* for complete listings.

Nightlife

Pubs, Bars, and Lounges

Bars or lounges are not traditional Prague fixtures; social life, of the drinking variety, usually takes place in pubs (*hospody*), which are liberally sprinkled throughout the city's neighborhoods. Tourists are welcome to join in the evening ritual of sitting around large tables and talking, smoking, and drinking beer in enormous quantities. Before venturing in, however, it's best to familiarize yourself with a few points of pub etiquette: First, always ask before sitting down if a chair is free. To order a beer (*pivo*), do not wave the waiter down or shout across the room; he will usually assume you want beer and bring it over to you without asking. He will also bring subsequent rounds to the table without asking. To refuse, just shake your head or say no thanks. At the end of the evening, usually around 10:30 or 11:00, the waiter will come to tally the bill. Some of the most popular pubs in the city center include **U Medvídků** (Na Perštýně 7), **U Vejvodů** (Jilská 4), and **U Zlatého Tygra** (Husova 17). All can get impossibly crowded.

An alternative to Prague's pubs are the few American-style bars that have sprung up during the past year. **Jo's Bar** (Malostranské nám. 7), one of the best and a haven for younger expats, serves bottled beer, mixed drinks, and good Mexican food. The **James Joyce Pub** (Liliova 10) and **Molly Malone's** (U obecního dvora 4) are authentically Irish, with Guinness on tap and excellent food. The major hotels also run their own bars and nightclubs. The **Piano Bar** (Hotel Palace, Panská 12) is the most pleasant of the lot; jacket and tie are suggested.

Cabaret

A multimedia extravaganza with actors, mime, and film is performed at **Laterna Magika** (Národní třída 4, Nové Město, tel. 02/2491-4129). Tickets range from 50 Kč. to 400 Kč. and sell out fast; the box office is open Monday 10-noon and 2–6 and Tuesday–Saturday 2–6. Noted Czech mime Boris Hybner performs nightly at 8 PM at the **Gag Studio** in the New Town (Národní 25, Nové Město, tel. 02/2422-9095). "Bohemian Fantasy," which performs May through October daily except Sunday at the **Alhambra** nightclub (Václavské nám. 5, tel. 02/2421-0463), is a glitzy, Las Vegas–style send-up of Bohemian history. Tickets cost $35–$50 and can be purchased at the Alhambra box office. For adult stage entertainment (with some nudity) try the **Lucerna Bar** (Štěpánská ul. 61, Nové Město) or **Varieté Praga** (Vodičkova ul. 30, Nové Město, tel. 02/2421-5945).

Discos

Dance clubs come and go with predictable regularity. The current favorite is **Radost FX** (Bělehradská 120, Prague 2, tel. 02/251210), featuring imported DJs playing the latest dance music and technopop from London. The café on the ground floor is open all night and serves wholesome vegetarian food. Two popular discos for dancing the night away with fellow tourists include **Lávka** (Novotného lávka 1, Staré Město, near the Charles Bridge) and the **Classic Club** (Pařížská 4, Staré Město, tel. 02/232-9191). The former features open-air dancing by the bridge on summer nights. Wenceslas Square is also packed with discos; the best strategy for finding the right place is simply to stroll the square and size up the crowds and the music.

Clubs catering to gay men and lesbians have blossomed in the past few years. Two of the most popular are the big, slightly raunchy **Riviera** (Národní 20, tel. 02/2491–2249) and the clean and classy **Mercury Club** (Kolínská 11, Prague 3, tel. 02/6731–0603).

Jazz Clubs

Jazz gained notoriety as a subtle form of protest under the Communists, and the city still has some great jazz clubs, featuring everything from swing to blues and modern. **Reduta** (Národní 20, tel. 02/2491–2246) features a full program of local and international musicians. **Agharta** (Krakovská 5, tel. 02/2421–2914) offers a variety of jazz acts in an intimate café/nightclub atmosphere. Music starts around 9 PM, but come earlier to get a seat. Traditional and Dixieland jazz can be heard nightly at the **Metropolitan Club** (Jungmannova 14, tel. 02/2421–6025). Names to watch for: Emil Viklický, a pianist reminiscent of Oscar Peterson who also plays compositions inspired by Moravian folk music; Vlasta Průchová, a singer whose backup quartet is made of top players; and Jiří Stivín, a good-humored flute-and-sax man doing straight-ahead modern jazz. Buy tickets well in advance for the **Original Prague Syncopated Orchestra,** which re-creates the look and sound of '20s and '30s dance bands, down to the microphones. Check posters around town or any of the English-language newspapers for current listings.

Rock Clubs

The year 1994 saw several well-known clubs in the center close down, leaving **RC Bunkr,** the first postrevolution underground club, still struggling to stay open (Lodecká 2, tel. 02/231–0735). Hard-rock enthusiasts should check out the **Rock Café** (Národní 20, tel. 02/2491–4416) or **Strahov 007** (near Strahov Stadium; tel. 02/520–777; Bus 143 or 176 to end of line). A trendy club-theater-café, the **Roxy,** reopened in 1994 presenting underground bands, jazz, and offbeat film and live theater (Dlouhá 33, tel. 02/231–6331). The **Malostranska Beseda** (Malostranské nám. 21, tel. 02/539024) and the **Belmondo Revival Club** (Bubenská 1, Prague 7, tel. 02/791–4854) are dependable bets for sometimes bizarre, but always good, musical acts from around the country.

Some of the best Czech bands are **Yo Yo Band,** which plays reggae with Czech lyrics; **Laura a jeji tygři,** a big, entertaining group with a horn section; **DG 307,** a remnant of the influential prerevolutionary underground scene; and the ska-influenced, dance-inducing **Sto zviřat.**

Among the favorite Czech folk groups are **Žalman a spol.** and the **Nedvěd brothers.** Concerts of modern folk and, during summer, revues presenting traditional Bohemian and Moravian music and dancing take place at the **Městká knihovna** (main public library, Mariánské nám., Staré Město).

Index

Notes

Notes

Fodor's Travel Guides

Available at bookstores everywhere, or call 1–800–533–6478, 24 hours a day.

U.S. Guides

Alaska

Arizona

Boston

California

Cape Cod, Martha's Vineyard, Nantucket

The Carolinas & the Georgia Coast

Chicago

Colorado

Florida

Hawaii

Las Vegas, Reno, Tahoe

Los Angeles

Maine, Vermont, New Hampshire

Maui

Miami & the Keys

New England

New Orleans

New York City

Pacific North Coast

Philadelphia & the Pennsylvania Dutch Country

The Rockies

San Diego

San Francisco

Santa Fe, Taos, Albuquerque

Seattle & Vancouver

The South

The U.S. & British Virgin Islands

USA

The Upper Great Lakes Region

Virginia & Maryland

Waikiki

Walt Disney World ar the Orlando Area

Washington, D.C.

Foreign Guides

Acapulco, Ixtapa, Zihuatanejo

Australia & New Zealand

Austria

The Bahamas

Baja & Mexico's Pacific Coast Resorts

Barbados

Berlin

Bermuda

Brittany & Normandy

Budapest

Canada

Cancún, Cozumel, Yucatán Peninsula

Caribbean

China

Costa Rica, Belize, Guatemala

The Czech Republic & Slovakia

Eastern Europe

Egypt

Euro Disney

Europe

Florence, Tuscany & Umbria

France

Germany

Great Britain

Greece

Hong Kong

India

Ireland

Israel

Italy

Japan

Kenya & Tanzania

Korea

London

Madrid & Barcelona

Mexico

Montréal & Québec City

Morocco

Moscow & St. Petersburg

The Netherlands, Belgium & Luxembourg

New Zealand

Norway

Nova Scotia, Prince Edward Island & New Brunswick

Paris

Portugal

Provence & the Riviera

Rome

Russia & the Baltic Countries

Scandinavia

Scotland

Singapore

South America

Southeast Asia

Spain

Sweden

Switzerland

Thailand

Tokyo

Toronto

Turkey

Vienna & the Danut Valley